The Persistence of Poverty in the United States

The Persistence of Poverty in the United States

Garth L. Mangum

Stephen L. Mangum

Andrew M. Sum

The Johns Hopkins University Press
Baltimore and London

The Johns Hopkins University Press
2715 North Charles Street
Baltimore, Maryland 21218-4363
www.press.jhu.edu

Library of Congress Cataloging-in-Publication Data

Mangum, Garth L.
   The persistence of poverty in the United States /
Garth L. Mangum, Stephen L. Mangum, and Andrew
M. Sum.
      p.   cm.
This work is partially based on "Programs in aid of the
poor" / Sar A. Levitan. 7th ed. 1998.
Includes bibliographical references and index.
   ISBN 0-8018-7130-1 (pbk. : alk. paper)
   1. Poor—United States.   2. Public welfare—United
States.   3. Economic assistance, Domestic—United
States.   I. Mangum, Stephen L.   II. Sum, Andrew.   III.
Levitan, Sar A. Programs in aid of the poor.   IV. Title.
HC 110.P6 M29   2003
362.5'2'0973—dc21   2002005370

A catalog record for this book is available from the
British Library.

Contents

Preface and Acknowledgments

This book is a total surprise to its authors, yet we trust readers will find it of value. We began preparing an eighth edition to *Programs in Aid of the Poor,* of which Sar Levitan had produced the first six editions from 1965 to 1990 and to which Garth Mangum and Steve Mangum had added a seventh edition in 1998. In the first chapter of each of those editions, the authors had summarized the incidence of poverty in the United States over the years since 1960, defining it, identifying its victims, and exploring its causes, before moving on in subsequent chapters to describe and assess the policies and programs designed to combat it. As we independently worked our way through the abundant available material for the introductory chapter of the eighth edition, we found ourselves with a combined first chapter of more than three hundred pages. We petitioned the long-suffering editors of the Johns Hopkins University Press, who had nursed *Programs in Aid of the Poor* over its nearly four decades, and were able to persuade them to publish a substantially shortened version of chapter 1 as this companion volume.

Programs in Aid of the Poor explores the substantial efforts made in these United States over the past nearly 40 years to help many individuals and families to survive despite their poverty and to enable others to rise out of poverty, aided by programs designed for those purposes. But this volume demonstrates more starkly than its parent the persistence of poverty in this nation. Though some individuals and families manage to escape it, the phenomenon diminishes not at all—or at least very little, except in times of persistent full employment, as occurred in the late years of the 1990s. Having been sobered by this thought, the student may ponder what more might conceivably be done to reduce the incidence of that endemic economic and social disease.

After defining poverty and asking why it is so persistent as a characteristic of the American economy and society (chapter 1), we discuss who the poor are (chapter 2) and where they live (chapter 3). In chapter 4 we explore the causes of poverty, and we return in more detail to the problems of poverty definition and measurement and their policy implications in chapter 5. Chapter 6 summarizes our findings and identifies some of the new strategies that U.S. antipoverty policy would have to undertake if a realistic "war on poverty" were to be launched. The reader is then referred to *Programs in Aid of the Poor* for an evaluation of existing antipoverty programs and detailed recommendations for programmatic and policy improvements.

The following scholars made major contributions to the chapters designated: Neeta Fogg (chapters 2 and 4), Joseph McLaughlin (chapter 3), and Mykhaylo Trub'skyy (chapters 2, 4, and 5). We are grateful to them for coauthorship of these chapters and to Sheila Palma for word processing and for managing the flow of materials from the multiplicity of participants.

We dedicate this volume to our departed friend and mentor, Sar A. Levitan.

The Persistence of Poverty in the United States

1. The Rediscovery of Poverty

After stressing the prevalence of affluence during the years imme-
diately following the Second World War, a coterie of social analysts, journalists, and politicians during the early 1960s rediscovered and began to publicize the persistence of poverty in the
United States. The findings of their studies, together with a set of
interrelated political developments, led to the formulation of a War
on Poverty by the federal government.[1] In his initial State of the
Union message in January 1964, President Lyndon B. Johnson reported to Congress and the nation that his administration "today,
here and now, declares unconditional war on poverty in America
. . . Our aim is not only to relieve the symptoms of poverty, but to
cure it and, above all, to prevent it."[2] Nearly 40 years later, the nation still has not won that war. In fact, if the relative length of the
measuring stick had not diminished over the subsequent years, as
discussed below, the American public would recognize both that
there are more poor people and poor families in the United States
today than in the 1960s and that the poverty rate is equally as high
as it was in the early 1970s, when the historical low was reached.

The War on Poverty

In the early 1960s the works of a diverse set of economists, social
commentators, and political activists, such as Robert Lampman,
Michael Harrington, and U.S. Senator Paul Douglas, awakened
Americans to the persistence of U.S. poverty. Harrington, in *The
Other America* (1962), called attention to the "invisible poor" in
both urban and rural areas, including migrant farmworkers, unemployed coal miners, white working poor trapped in depressed
manufacturing towns, inner city black poor, and the socially isolated elderly poor.[3] Though he never rigorously defined poverty,
Harrington estimated a likely U.S. population of 40 to 50 million

poor in the late 1950s. Harrington's book received substantial pub-
licity from a lengthy review in the *New Yorker* magazine by Dwight
McDonald in early 1963. The review article supposedly came to
the attention of President John F. Kennedy, who had first viewed
poverty face to face in West Virginia during his 1960 campaign,
and of Walter Heller, chairman of the President's Council of Economic Advisers. President Kennedy called upon the council for a
formal study of poverty in the United States in preparation for a
possible antipoverty initiative during the 1964 campaign, which
he never had the opportunity to pursue. Upon becoming president,
Johnson was briefed on the study and, feeling himself to have considerable personal familiarity with the topic, decided to take it on
as a primary federal initiative.

That the newly declared war would turn out to be a long series
of skirmishes could have been predicted by noting the internal instructions to those assigned to inventory and marshal the available
federal arsenal: the initiative was not to cost more than an additional $3 billion beyond existing relevant expenditures for at least
the first fiscal year in order to avoid pushing the federal budget beyond $100 billion for the first time. The weapons were to be pri-
marily employment and training programs—the poor were to be
enabled to earn their way out of poverty. The Economic Opportunity Act of 1964 introduced the Neighborhood Youth Corps, offering work experience and earnings to youth from low-income families. The Job Corps established residential training centers for
youth from dysfunctional homes and neighborhoods, using primarily idle military and forestry facilities. The Community Action
Program was expected to enable maximum participation of the
poor in local policy decisions concerning their economic and social betterment. The Manpower Development and Training Act, introduced in 1962 to retrain experienced workers displaced by economic and technological change, was modified to provide initial
skill training and remedial education to those never adequately
prepared for employment. Federal matching aid to state vocational
education was expanded and reoriented. The pursuit of Equal Employment Opportunity was undertaken to remove labor market
discrimination as an obstacle to earning one's way out of poverty.
The Head Start program was introduced to better enable children
from poverty-stricken homes to keep up with others in elementary
school. In 1965, education reform was undertaken through the Elementary and Secondary Education Act to help schools affected by
poverty to prepare children and youth for life. Modest health,
housing, and community development programs were added.

The fact was recognized that direct cash payments to the poor totaling $12 billion would bring every family's income up to the newly established poverty line, assuming that the availability of this additional unearned income would not reduce their self-reliance. But this alternative was not given serious consideration. The only income maintenance initiative was to change the Aid to Dependent Children (ADC) provision of the Social Security Act of 1935 to Aid to Families with Dependent Children (AFDC). The former had been designed to support families that had lost their male breadwinner, enabling the widowed mother to stay home to care for her children. Now, states were authorized to cover two-parent families when the father was unable to find employment. One-half of the states chose to do so. Many of the initial programs underwent change, and others were added, but the employment and earnings emphasis of the War on Poverty continued. Unforeseen changes in family structure, personal conduct, and personal attitudes toward welfare would subsequently multiply the public assistance component far beyond the employment and training component, but that was never the original intent.

Counting the Poor

Who were these poor for whom the war on poverty was to be fought? Rigorous definitions of poverty were essential to establish eligibility for assistance and to measure progress in achieving antipoverty goals. Alternative definitions and measures are discussed in chapter 5. Suffice it to say here that a 1955 Department of Agriculture survey had shown that the average American family—not just the poor—spent one-third of its budget on food. The Department of Agriculture also had derived alternative family food budgets from among which a minimal one was chosen. This food budget, varying by family size, was multiplied by 3 to become the threshold between poverty and nonpoverty. This "economy food plan" has been etched in stone since the 1960s; the federal measure of poverty advances annually only as a result of changes in the rate of inflation for consumer goods and services as measured by the U.S. Bureau of Labor Statistics's Consumer Price Index for All Urban Consumers (CPI-U) (table 1.1).

The official definition of poverty, with all of its limitations, provides a means of determining how many and what proportion of the U.S. population has been poor over the years. Figure 1.1 shows trends in the poverty rate and the number of poor people from 1959 to 2000.

Table 1.1. Weighted Average Poverty Thresholds for Nonfarm Families by Family Size, Selected Years, 1959–2000

Family Size	1959	1970	1980	1989	1995	1999	2000
1	$1,467	$1,954	$4,190	$6,310	$7,763	$8,501	$8,959
2	1,894	2,525	5,363	8,076	9,933	10,869	11,531
3	2,324	3,099	6,565	9,885	12,158	13,290	13,470
4	2,973	3,968	8,414	12,674	15,569	17,029	17,761
5	3,506	4,680	9,966	14,990	18,408	20,127	21,419
6	3,944	5,260	11,269	16,921	20,804	22,727	24,636
7	4,849	6,468	12,761	19,162	23,552	24,802	28,347
8	na	na	14,199	21,328	26,237	28,967	31,704
≥9	na	na	16,896	25,480	31,280	34,417	38,138

Source: U.S. Census Bureau.

Fig. 1.1. Trends in the Number of Poor Persons and Poverty Rates: United States, 1959 to 2000

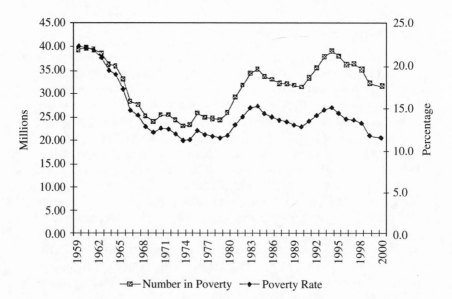

Source: U.S. Census Bureau, Current Population Reports, Series P60-No. 210

Persons in Poverty

After falling substantially between 1959 and 1969 and then staying at the lower level until the late 1970s, the number of poor in the United States rose and fluctuated at a level not far below the 1959 numbers until the economic boom of the late 1990s. After all, the U.S. population was much larger in 2000 than it was in 1959. The poverty rate also declined sharply between 1959 and 1973, the Golden Era of the U.S. economy.[4] Thereafter, it fell no further, despite the governmental war on poverty, and fluctuated with the business cycle. From 22.4 percent in 1959, the poverty rate fell to 11.1 percent in 1973, the lowest point ever measured, rose to 12.3 percent in 1975, fell back to 11.7 percent in 1979, and then rose to 15.2 percent in 1983 after the back-to-back economic recessions of 1980 and 1981–82. The number of poor persons rose by more than 9 million between 1979 and 1983. Strong economic and job growth combined with declining unemployment over the 1982–89 period helped lower the poverty rate back down to 12.8 percent by 1989, after which the 1990–91 recession drove it back up to 15.1 percent. There was slow recovery through 1995. Thereafter, real wage growth (including wage increases for workers at the bottom of the distribution), steep declines in unemployment, and the absence of further increases in income inequality helped push the poverty rate down steadily to 11.3 percent by 2000, the lowest rate of persons in poverty since 1978 but still modestly higher than the 11.1 percent rate in 1973. Numerically, there were 31.1 million poor persons in the nation in 2000, up from the low of 23.0 million in 1973. What will happen to poverty rates in the softening economy since 2001 remains to be seen, although past experience would suggest at least a temporary halt to any further progress in poverty reduction.

Trends in Family Poverty Rates

Poverty rates of U.S. families over the past 40 years have closely mirrored those for the entire resident population (figure 1.2). Between 1959 and 1973, the rate of poverty among the nation's families declined by more than half from 18.5 percent to 8.8 percent. The 1973 rate of family poverty represented the historical low for the nation until 2000, when the nation's family poverty rate fell to 8.6 percent. Since 1974, family poverty rates have continued to vary over the business cycle but have exhibited no long-term decline. During the recessionary and inflationary environment of the early 1980s, the family poverty rate rose sharply from 9.2 percent

Fig. 1.2. Number and Percentage of Poor Families in the United States, 1959 to 2000

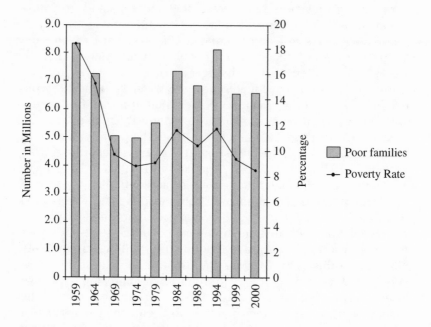

Source: U.S. Census Bureau, Current Population Reports

in 1979 to 12.3 percent in 1983. During the next six years, the poverty rate declined to 10.3 percent as a consequence of rising real family incomes and declining unemployment but did not return to its 1979 rate, largely as a consequence of increasing family income inequality. The share of aggregate family income captured by the bottom one-fifth of families declined from 5.4 percent to 4.6 percent over the 1980s.

During the 1990–91 recession and the "jobless recovery" of 1991–92, the family poverty rate steadily increased, peaking at 12.3 percent in 1993, with just under 8.4 million families classified as poor in that year. Over the following seven years, sustained growth in real family incomes, strong growth in employment, steep declines in unemployment, and a modest improvement in the share of income captured by the bottom one-fifth of families allowed the family poverty rate to decline steadily to 8.6 percent by 2000. The 8.6 percent official poverty rate among U.S. families in 2000 was a new historical low, slightly below the previous low achieved in 1973 and 1974, and there were 6.2 million poor families in 2000, a total that was 1.4 million higher than the number of poor families in 1973. After declining substantially between 1959 and 1973, a persistent new poverty plateau emerged: one out of every seven or eight persons and one out of every nine to ten families.

Poverty's Gap and Depth

The poverty count merely shows how many residents are in households with incomes below the poverty threshold. It does not measure how poor they are. The poverty gap—the difference between the actual family income of the poor and the poverty line—is one measure of the degree of poverty. Despite the narrowing of the average gap between 1959 and 1967, it has widened persistently since (table 1.2). Thus, while there are fewer poor families as a proportion of the population now, their poverty is deeper than in the past. As noted earlier, at the beginning of the antipoverty effort in 1964, the federal government calculated that an additional $12 billion given to all families in poverty without their reducing their work effort would have brought every family up to the poverty line. That total poverty gap would have been $50.5 billion in 1994 and $42.4 billion in 2000.

The number and percentage of persons with incomes below 50 percent of the poverty threshold is another measure of poverty's depth (table 1.3). The persistence of a high percentage and number of poor persons with such low money incomes since 1983 while the overall percentage and number of the poor fluctuated suggests the existence of a hard core of poor persons who remain resistant to antipoverty efforts while others move in and out of the poverty ranks.

Table 1.2. Average Poverty Gap, 1967–1999 (Income in 1999 Dollars)

Year	Families	Persons Not in Families
1959	$6,608	$4,390
1967	5,901	3,632
1973	5,910	3,499
1979	6,188	3,428
1989	6,574	3,813
1995	6,601	4,113
1999	6,687	4,206

Source: U.S. Census Bureau as analyzed by Mishel, Bernstein, and Schmitt, *The State of Working America, 2000–2001*, p. 300.

Table 1.3. Persons with Incomes below 50 Percent of the Poverty Level, 1975–2000

Year	% of All Poor	No. of Persons
1975	29.9%	7,733,000
1979	32.8	8,553,000
1983	38.5	13,590,000
1989	38.0	11,983,000
1995	38.1	13,892,000
1999	39.3	12,681,000
2000	39.0	12,158,000

Source: Mishel, Bernstein, and Schmitt, *The State of Working America, 2000–2001,* p. 302, and authors' data.

Each of these measures of poverty demonstrates the common pattern of notable decline during the 1960s and early 1970s with marked persistence thereafter.

Measurement Problems

All of the above findings are based on the official poverty index. Measurement problems greatly affect one's assessment of the extent to which the national war on poverty has been successfully waged. In an era when the average family spends one-seventh of its income on food, the nation still uses an official poverty index established on the assumption that the average appetite absorbs one-third of income. Housing costs, which were in the mid-1960s assumed to account for one-quarter of the low-income budget, were at the end of the 1990s closer to one-third and rising for the average family and closer to one-half for the majority of low-income households unable to receive rental housing assistance. Multiplying the cost of that original 1950s–60s food basket by 7 would more than double the poverty threshold, placing the poverty rate back above its 1959 level. But how relevant is that food basket measurement in a new century? When it was established in the mid-1960s, the poverty threshold was approximately equal to one-half the median post-tax income for a four-person family.[5] In 1999, the poverty line for a four-person family was equal to only one-third of the median post-tax income for four-person families. If the poverty line were restored to 50 percent of median post-tax income, where it was in 1964, 56.8 million people would have been considered poor in 1999 rather than the 32.3 million measured as poor in that year by the current criterion. The poverty line for a

four-person family in 1999 would have been $29,990 rather than
$17,029. In 1998, rather than 12.7 percent, the poverty rate for per-
sons would have been 22.3 percent, almost equal to its 1959 level.
The official poverty measure based on food costs could be characterized as an absolute measure of poverty, and the relationship to
the median income could be called relative poverty. Chapter 5 explores the implications of the obsolescence of the official poverty
rate.

The same phenomenon exists from the vantage point of the family or of the individual (see table 1.4). Leaving aside questions of
adjustments due to family size, the family income in current dollars equal to one-half of the median income for all U.S. families
ranged from $2,708 in 1959 to $24,475 in 1999. In constant dollars,
the value of one-half of the median family income rose from
$14,280 in 1959 to $24,475 in 1999, a gain of 71 percent. Over those
40 years, the share of U.S. families with pretax incomes below 50
percent of the median family income fluctuated over a fairly narrow range from a low of 18.8 percent in 1969 to a high of 22.4 percent in 1992.

Given the fact that the number of families in the United States
increased from 45 million to 72 million over those same 40 years,
there was a considerably greater number of families (15.8 million)
experiencing relative poverty in 1999 than in 1959 (9.1 million).

**Table 1.4. Number and Percentage of U.S. Families with Money
Incomes below 50 Percent of the Median Income of All U.S.
Families, Selected Years, 1959–1999**

Year	50% of Median Income	No. of Families (1000s)	% of Families
1959	$2,708	9,112	20.2%
1962	2,978	9,506	20.2
1965	3,478	9,653	19.9
1969	4,717	9,684	18.9
1973	6,026	10,900	19.8
1977	8,004	11,443	20.0
1979	9,794	11,850	19.9
1982	11,716	12,769	20.8
1985	13,867	13,156	20.7
1989	17,106	14,407	21.8
1992	18,286	15,280	22.4
1995	20,306	15,172	21.8
1999	24,475	15,847	22.0

Whether measured from an absolute or a relative vantage point, therefore, the numbers and rates of family poverty in the United States were higher in 1999 than they were in 1973, one decade after the start of the official antipoverty effort in the mid-1960s.

Other problems with the official poverty measure are discussed in greater detail in chapter 5. None of the noncash goods, services, and other benefits (such as food stamps, health care, and subsidized housing) nor the earned income tax credits introduced subsequently as contributions to the nation's antipoverty efforts are counted as income in the poverty measures. Their effects are also discussed in chapter 5, but they are aids to those in poverty, not potential measures of escape from it. Their existence does not change the fact of poverty's persistence in the United States. To some extent, we have prosecuted our war against poverty somewhat the way Senator George Aiken of Vermont advised that we prosecute the war in Vietnam: "Declare victory and go home." However, the war against poverty has not been abandoned. Its skirmishes continue with widely fluctuating commitment.

What Is Being Done?

The biblical admonition "the poor shall never cease out of the land" can be read either as a pessimistic forecast or as an acknowledgment that each society defines poverty in its own terms as living standards change over time. By official U.S. standards, consistently but with cyclical fluctuations, about one American in eight has been considered poor according to government statistics for the past 30 years. Using the original relative income standards of 1964, that ratio is more like one in five. In no other developed country is the poverty rate as high as in the United States.[6] Nevertheless, even the lowest-income families in this country are rarely confronted with the specter of starvation, though many have inadequate diets. On the other hand, in the underdeveloped countries of the world, poverty is equated with living at the brink of subsistence. The World Bank currently uses as its worldwide poverty indicator a per capita income of one dollar a day, a level of living that would be incomprehensible in developed country terms. A persistent question in any viable democracy must always be, To what extent should people be left untrammeled in their pursuit of their own economic well-being, and to what extent should the society be responsible for assisting those left behind in that struggle for the "good life"?

That is essentially the topic of a companion volume to this work entitled *Programs in Aid of the Poor,*[7] which describes and assesses antipoverty programs in the United States. The fact that the poverty measure is faulty or even that poverty in the United States remains inordinately high by the standards of the developed world does not mean that the almost 40-year war on poverty has been lacking in weapons, battles, or successes. Nevertheless, the basic fact remains that, if the same measures were being used today as were derived and applied in 1964, the poverty rate would be no lower now than it was nearly 40 years earlier and the numbers of persons in poverty would be far higher than previously. The best that can be said for the unconditional war on poverty is that without it conditions would have been worse. The skirmishes against poverty continue. The primary purpose of this book is to assess, at the turn of the millennium, the status of what may be the modern equivalent of the Hundred Years' War of the Middle Ages.

2. A Demographic Profile of the Nation's Poor

Knowledge of the demographic characteristics of the poor is essential to an understanding of the persistence of poverty in the United States. This chapter provides a statistical profile of the changing demographic characteristics of the poor, including their age distribution, their race and ethnicity, their nativity status, and their household living arrangements.

The Age Composition of the Poor

The age composition of the nation's resident, noninstitutional population and that of its poor have changed markedly in opposite directions over the past 40 years. At the end of the 1950s, persons under 18 years of age accounted for 36.4 percent of the population, and their share rose further to just under 37 percent at the tail end of the births to the baby boom generation in the early 1960s. As the members of the baby boom generation were replaced by the baby bust generation, the share of the nation's population represented by children under 18 declined steadily, falling to 26 percent in 1989 and remaining in the 26–27 percent range throughout the 1990s. The movement of the baby boom generation into their early 20s beginning in the late 1960s helped boost the share of the nation's population comprising 18- to 64-year-olds. Their share of the population rose from 55 percent in 1959 to just under 62 percent in 1989 and remained there throughout the 1990s. Given historically lower poverty rates among this age group, their rising share of the population should have contributed to a lower incidence of poverty problems among the nation's population since the late 1960s.

Among these three age groups, the largest relative increase in the nation's population since 1959 took place in people 65 and older. Bolstered by increases in their life expectancy, the number of residents ages 65 and older more than doubled from 1959 to 1999, rising from 15.6 million to 36.6 million, thereby increasing their share of the population from 8.8 percent in 1959 to 12.0 percent in 1989 but dropping to 11.9 percent by 1999. The entry of the Depression-era birth cohort into the ranks of the elderly beginning in the mid-1990s helped slow down the growth of the nation's elderly population; however, their numbers will begin to grow rapidly from 2010 onward as the early members of the baby boom generation enter the ranks of the elderly.

Between 1959 and 1973, poverty rates among members of each of these age groups declined by one-half or more. However, since 1973, the only age group that has experienced a generally steady decline in its poverty rate is the elderly, which dropped below the poverty rate of the rest of the population in 1982 and has remained there since (figure 2.1). Nonelderly adults (18–64) came to represent a majority of the nation's poor (53%) in 1999 because of a combination of a large increase in their population fueled by the aging of the baby boomers, high levels of foreign immigration in the 1980s and 1990s, and the inability of members of this age group to lower their poverty rates back to the historical low reached in 1973. Noting that, starting in the mid-1970s, the poverty rate of the elderly had fallen below that of children, former New York Senator Daniel Patrick Moynihan asserted that "it is fair to assume that

Fig. 2.1. The Age Composition of the Poor in the United States, 1969 and 1999

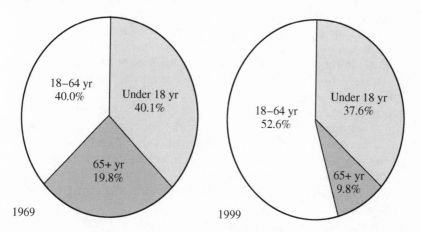

Source: U.S. Census Bureau, Current Population Survey, Historical Tables—People—table 3

the United States has become the first society in history in which a person is more likely to be poor if young rather than old."[1]

Trends in the Child Poverty Rate, 1959–2000

Although nearly one in six children were poor in 2000, this was the lowest rate of child poverty since the early 1970s, when the poverty rate of related children under 18 had declined to 14.2 percent in 1973 (figure 2.2). After declining steeply during the 1960s and early 1970s, the child poverty rate increased substantially during the 1980s. Despite the strong economic expansion during the 1982–89 period, the poverty rate of children remained quite high, declining by only 2 percentage points, from 21 percent at the trough of the business cycle in 1982 to 19 percent at the time of the cyclical peak in 1989. During the period of recession and slow job growth of the early 1990s, the poverty rate among children increased steadily, rising to 22 percent in 1993 before declining to 15.7 percent by 2000, a reduction of nearly 6.3 percentage points (or 28%).

The depth and persistence of child poverty, with the poverty rate of children under the age of six being much higher than that of school-aged children, is the most chilling factor on the antipoverty scene. Children who spend large periods of their childhood in poverty experience adverse long-term consequences on their academic achievement, educational attainment, health, criminal justice behavior, and social behavior far into their adult lives. Children who were raised in poor families are more likely to lag in cognitive development, have lower levels of academic achievement and aspirations, repeat grades, and have more conduct problems in school. Research has also found these traits to be precursors of delinquency, the decision to drop out of school before obtaining a high school diploma, adolescent parenthood and joblessness, and intermittent employment on into adulthood. If these consequences materialize, many poor children will become poor adults with low levels of education and other forms of human capital, accompanied by limited attachment to the labor market. Early parenthood added to limited earning capacity often transforms the children of poverty into dependent and destitute parents producing another generation of poor children and continuing the intergenerational cycle of poverty.[2]

Poverty rates among related children under 18 who live in female-headed families are particularly startling, although some important progress has been made in recent years. Their poverty rate

Fig. 2.2. Trends in the Poverty Rate of Related Children under 18 Residing in All Families and in Female-headed Families, 1959–1999

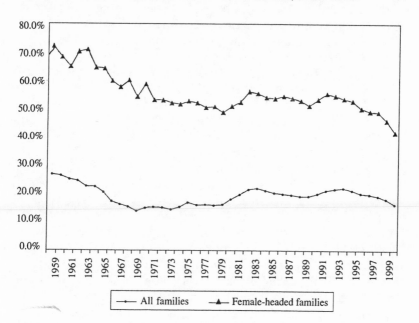

Source: U.S. Census Bureau, Current Population Survey, Historical Tables—People—table 3

declined from 72 percent in 1959 to 49 percent in 1979, a steep decline of 23 percentage points over this 20-year period that still left nearly one-half in poverty. During the recession of the early 1980s, the child poverty rate in female-headed families peaked at 56 percent; it then declined to 51 percent by 1989 and then rose again to 54 percent by 1993. Between 1993 and 1999, the poverty rate of these children declined by nearly 12 percentage points to the lowest point in over 40 years. Nevertheless, 42 out of every 100 related children residing in female-headed families remained poor in 1999. Children residing in female-headed families were more than 5 times more likely to be poor in 1999 than were their counterparts who lived in married-couple families (42% vs. 8%). Children who lived in male-headed families (with no wife present in the household) also were more likely to be poor than were children residing in married-couple families, but they were less than half as likely to be poor as their counterparts who resided in female-headed families. Increases in the proportion of children residing in female-headed families clearly underlie a major part of the increased rate of child poverty in the United States. In fact, a study that compared the 1971 marital status of men and women to that in 1989 concluded that all of the increase in child poverty between 1971 and 1989 was attributable to the rise in one-parent families in the United States over that period.[3]

The rates of child poverty among female-headed families also vary widely by the marital status of the householder—previously married (and now widowed, separated, or divorced) or never married. A study based on the 1997 National Survey of America's Families found that, even after controlling for a mother's characteristics (including her education, age at birth, and employment status), children who were born to unmarried mothers were more likely be poor than were other children in single-mother families.[4] Over 56 percent of related children under 18 who lived in these types of families were poor in 1999. In contrast, only one-third of all related children under 18 who lived with female householders who were widowed, divorced, or separated were poor in 1999. Children living with a never-married, single female householder were 70 percent more likely to be poor than were other children living in female-headed families. There are other important differences in the poverty rates of children living in female-headed families in different marital statuses. Children of separated female householders were at considerably higher risk of poverty relative to children of divorced female householders (48% vs. 29%). The poverty rate of children residing with widowed women, who often have access to their deceased husband's pension or receive survivor's benefits, was slightly lower (26%) than that of children living with a female divorced householder.

One of the factors that underlie the differences in the economic status of female-headed families is the receipt of child support income. Child support payments offer an additional source of income to female-headed families and, depending on the size of the payments, they could serve as an effective antipoverty tool for these families.[5] Divorced women are considerably more likely to receive some child support income than are separated or never-married women. In 1999, 47 percent of the divorced female family heads with related children under 18 reported receiving some child support payment during the year, compared to 29 percent of separated women and only 22 percent of never-married women. When they do receive child support income, divorced women receive larger amounts of income than do their separated or never-married counterparts. In 1999, the mean child support income of divorced women was $5,400, an amount that was 23 percent higher than the average child support income of separated women ($4,400) and twice the mean child support income received by never-married women ($2,700).

Receipt of child support income has a substantive effect on the child poverty rate in female-headed families. Nearly 42 percent of all related children residing in female-headed families were poor in 1999. The child poverty rate among children residing in female-headed families where the householder reported that she had received some child support income during the year was approximately 27 percent, or 15 percentage points lower than that of all related children in female-headed families. Among single female householders who did not receive any child support payments during 1999, the child poverty rate was 48 percent, nearly 22 percentage points higher than the poverty rate among female-headed families that received some child support income. The poverty rate among all children in female-headed families would have been nearly 3 percentage points higher (44.7%) and among all families receiving child support 10 percentage points higher (36%) in the absence of any child support income. In 1999, there were 6.6 million poor related children under 18 residing in female-headed families in the United States. Excluding child support income from these families' total income would have raised the total number of poor children in female-headed families to just over 7 million. Thus, in 1999, child support income enabled 422,000 poor children, or 6 percent of all potentially poor children in female-headed families, to climb out of poverty during that year.[6]

Children living in families with better-educated householders also are much less likely to be poor than are children living with poorly educated family householders. In 1999, the child poverty rate in families with a householder who was a high school dropout was 42 percent compared to only 2.5 percent in families with a householder who had completed four or more years of college. Nearly 1 in 5 (19%) children in a household headed by a high school graduate were poor compared to 1 in 10 children who lived in a family headed by someone who had completed some postsecondary education but had not earned a bachelor's degree. Because better-educated householders are more able to secure full-time, year-round jobs and garner higher wages in the labor market, their families have higher incomes and lower poverty rates. Better-educated persons are also more likely to have full-time jobs with benefits, such as health insurance coverage, pensions, paid vacations, and the like. Most poorly educated householders unfortunately are relegated to the lower skill segment of the labor market, which is characterized by lower wages, more frequent part-time employment, and few work-related benefits.

The accelerated pace of immigration during the 1990s was a substantial contributor to poverty among the U.S. population. Immigrants who have recently entered the United States are much more likely than native-born Americans to be poorly educated and to possess lower levels of literacy proficiencies and occupational skills. Moreover, the recent wave of immigrants is more likely to consist of persons who possess limited English language proficiency. These human capital traits pose sizable labor market barriers that frequently restrict employment to the low-skill and low-wage sector of the economy. Poverty rates among immigrant families and children residing in those families are higher than those of children residing in families of U.S.-born householders. According to a recent study by the Urban Institute, children of immigrants also were 40 percent more likely to live in families with food-related problems, 2.3 times more likely to live in families with housing cost burdens in excess of 50 percent, 4 times more likely to live in crowded housing, and twice as likely to be uninsured and in poor health compared to children of U.S.-born parents.[7] Figure 2.3 illustrates some of these factors that influence poverty rates.

Analysis of the poverty rates of children under 18 by the nativity status of the family householder reveals a 72 percent higher poverty rate among children in foreign-born families (24.9%) compared to the poverty rate of children who lived in families with a U.S.-born householder (14.6%). There also were large differences in the child poverty rate among immigrant families classified by the year of entry of the householder into the United States. Nearly one out of three children residing in families of recent immigrants (who arrived between 1990 and 1999) were poor in 1999, compared to 22 percent of related children who lived in families of immigrants who arrived before 1990.

Changes in Child Poverty Rates, 1992–1999

Although the overall child poverty rate declined substantially between 1992 and 1999, the absolute rates of decline in child poverty rates varied by the characteristics of the family householder. Be-

Fig. 2.3. Poverty Rates of Related Children under 18 by Selected Characteristics of the Family Householder, 1999

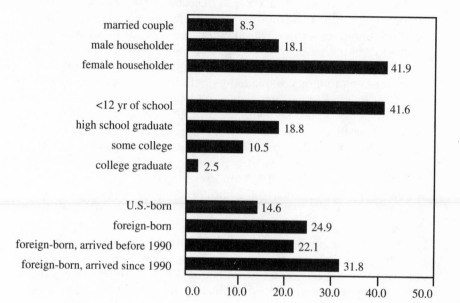

Source: March Current Population Survey 2000 public use data tapes, tabulations by the authors

tween 1992 and 1999, the poverty rate among all related children under 18 declined from 21.4 percent to 16.3 percent. Among the three types of families, the largest absolute decline in the child poverty rate occurred among female-headed families, down from 55 percent in 1992 to 42 percent in 1999. While the absolute decline in the child poverty rate varied by family type, the relative sizes of the declines in child poverty rates between 1992 and 1999 were the same across each of the three family types, about 23 percent. Even after declining steadily between 1992 and 1999, the child poverty rate remained about 5 times higher among children in female-headed families than among children in married-couple families.

The largest absolute declines in child poverty rates between 1992 and 1999 occurred among children residing with family householders who were high school dropouts, as low unemployment rates brought employment opportunities to those ordinarily left behind. The poverty rate among children living in families with poorly educated householders declined from 50.4 percent in 1992 to 41.6 percent in 1999, a 9-percentage point decline. The poverty rate among children residing with householders who were college graduates, which was already quite low in 1992, declined modestly to 2.5 percent in 1999. There were 4- and 2-percentage point declines in the child poverty rates, respectively, among children residing in families headed by a high school graduate and in families headed by a person who had completed some postsecondary schooling but not earned a bachelor's degree.

Child poverty rates are much higher in families headed by a single female, in families headed by poorly educated persons, and among immigrant families. There are two main factors underlying this phenomenon. First, these families in general are at a substantially higher risk of poverty. Second, poorly educated families and immigrant families tend to have an above average number of related children under 18. On average, poor families have more children than nonpoor families. In 1999, the average number of related children residing in families headed by a high school dropout who had at least one related child under 18 was 2.1. In the same year, the average number of children in families headed by a college graduate was 1.83. Thus, the average number of children in families headed by high school dropouts was 15 percent higher than that of their college graduate counterparts. Immigrant families had an average of 1.99 children compared to a mean of 1.86 among families with a U.S.-born householder, a 7 percent difference. The mean number of children in poor families was 22 percent higher than the mean number of children in nonpoor families.

Partly as a consequence of these variations in the mean number of children per family, poor children are disproportionately concentrated in certain types of families. The distribution of all children and poor related children under 18 by different types of families is presented in table 2.1. These data can be used to identify the degree of concentration of poor children in certain types of families. The share of all poor children under 18 who lived in families with a householder with fewer than 12 years of schooling was 2.5 times higher than the share of all related children under 18 who lived with a householder who was a high school dropout. Families with high school graduate householders also had modestly disproportionate numbers of poor children residing in them. In contrast, families with a householder who had completed at least some postsecondary schooling accounted for a below average share

Table 2.1. Percentage Distribution of Related Children under 18 by Family Type and by Educational Attainment and Nativity of the Family Householder, 1999

Characteristic of the Family or Householder	(A) All	(B) Poor	(C) Ratio (B)/(A)
All	100%	100%	—
Educational attainment			
Less than 12 years	17.1	43.5	2.544
High school graduate	30.3	34.9	1.152
Some college	27.8	17.8	0.640
College graduate	24.8	3.8	0.153
Nativity status			
U.S. born	16.5	25.1	1.521
Foreign born	83.5	74.9	0.897
Type of family			
Married couple	72.8	37.1	0.510
Male headed	4.8	5.3	1.104
Female headed	22.4	57.7	2.576

Source: March Current Population Survey 2000 public use data tapes, tabulations by the authors.

of poor children. Nearly 28 percent of all children lived in families with householders who had completed some postsecondary schooling (but no bachelor's degree) compared to only 18 percent of poor children who lived in such families. In 1999, one-quarter of all children lived in a family headed by a four-year college graduate, whereas fewer than 4 percent of all poor children were members of such families. Children living in families headed by a high school dropout were, thus, 17 times as likely to be poor as their peers living in families headed by a four-year college graduate. Children in families headed by immigrants also were over-represented among the ranks of the poor. The share of poor children in foreign-born families was 52 percent higher than the share of all related children who lived in these families.

There also were sizable differences in the living arrangements of all children and poor children by type of family. In 1999, nearly 73 percent of all related children lived in married-couple families, but only 37 percent of all poor related children were members of a married-couple family. The proportion of poor children residing in male-headed families (no female spouse present) was 10 percent larger than the proportion of all children residing in these families. Poor children were disproportionately concentrated in female-headed families with no male spouse present. In 1999, while 22 percent of all related children under 18 lived in single-parent, female-headed families, these families were home to nearly 60 percent of all poor related children under the age of 18. The growth in the number of female-headed families with children combined with high levels of poverty among female-headed families has exacerbated the problem of the "feminization of poverty" (i.e., the growing share of all poor persons who are single women and their children). Poor children have become increasingly concentrated in female-headed families. In 1959, only 9 percent of all related children under 18 lived in female-headed families, and 24 percent of all poor related children lived in female-headed families, a difference of 15 percentage points. By 1999, the difference between these two proportions had grown to over 35 percentage points, 22.4 percent for all children compared to 57.7 percent for poor children. The latter two percentages had declined further to 21.7 percent and 55.2 percent by 2000.

The favorable trends in child poverty rates during the economic expansion of the 1990s were at the same time both impressive and sobering. The child poverty rate declined during the 1992–2000 period from 22 percent to 16 percent. In 2000, the poverty rate of related children under 18 in the United States was at its lowest level since the mid-1970s. Over the same time period, the sharpest declines in child poverty rates have been among the most vulnerable group of children. Nevertheless, one of every six children in the nation was still poor by the official poverty standard in 2000. Certain subgroups of children continue to have poverty rates over 40 percent even after the sizable declines that took place during the last half of the 1990s.

Since most of the progress was made among children in the most vulnerable groups of families, there is a risk that part of these gains will have reversed as the economy slowed after 2000. The most poverty-prone families typically are headed by young women who are poorly educated and have a poor employment history and limited work experience. The economic expansion of the 1990s helped a growing number of these families climb out of poverty. But many are still on the edge of poverty, just one paycheck, or an illness, or even a major car repair away from being pushed back into poverty. They also occupy jobs at the bottom of the labor market queue and with their reduced seniority are at an above average risk of losing their jobs as the economy declines.

Poverty among the Elderly

As noted earlier, the nation's elderly population has experienced the most substantial absolute and relative declines in its poverty rate over the past 40 years. Between 1959 and 1973, the poverty rate among the elderly was reduced by half, going from 35.2 percent to 16.3 percent. By 1999, their poverty rate had declined to 9.7 percent, the lowest of our three age groups. In fact, between 1959 and 1999, the poverty rate of the elderly went from being the highest to being the lowest, although it did rise back to 10.2 percent in 2000.

The sharp decline in the incidence of poverty problems among the nation's elderly over the past 40 years was substantially influenced by a more rapid growth in the median real incomes of elderly households and persons.[8] Between 1967 and 1999, the median real income of households headed by an elderly individual rose from $12,667 to $22,812, a gain of 80 percent versus an increase of only 24 percent for all households across the country over the same period. The relative income position of elderly households improved nearly steadily over this 32-year period, rising from 38 percent of the median for all households in 1967 to just under 57 percent in 1993, before declining slightly to 56 percent by 1999.

The substantial reductions in poverty among the elderly population since the late 1950s are not attributable to improved labor market prospects and earnings among elderly men or women. While 42 percent of older men (65+) were active in the labor force in 1950, only 17 percent were by 1995.[9] The strength of the national economy in the mid- to late 1990s, with its growing labor shortages and rising real wages, helped attract only a few older men and women back into the labor market. In 2000, the annual average labor force participation rates of elderly men and women were 17.5 percent and 9.4 percent, respectively, only 0.6 to 0.7 percentage points above the rates that prevailed at mid-decade.

The ability of the nation's elderly to avoid poverty problems over the past 40 years is primarily attributable to the effects of the Social Security retirement program and other cash income transfers for the elderly, including the federal-state Supplemental Security Income Program for the Aged and the Disabled. Increased real benefits to Social Security retirees over the years plus the effects of adjusting benefits each year for changes in the cost-of-living index as measured by the Consumer Price Index for All Urban Consumers (CPI-U price index) have boosted the real incomes

of many elderly households above the poverty line. In the absence
of all cash government transfers, including Social Security retirement, the poverty rates of elderly Americans would be considerably higher. For example, if we exclude all cash government transfers from the incomes of all elderly households, the poverty rate
among persons 65–74 years old would rise from 9 to 41 percent
and the poverty rate among those 75 and older would rise by a multiple of 5, from 10.7 percent to 56.0 percent. In contrast, the receipt
of cash government transfers by families containing children has
a much lower effect in reducing the rate of poverty among such
children—there is only a 14 percent reduction compared to 78 percent for the 65- to 74-year-olds and 81 percent for those over 74.

The poverty rates of the nation's elderly population do, however, continue to vary by gender, family living arrangements, and
race and ethnicity. In 1999, elderly women were 70 percent more
likely to be poor than were elderly men (12% vs. 7%), largely reflecting the higher rates of poverty among and greater numbers of
women who live alone. The elderly who live in families (with their
spouses or children) were much less likely to be poor—5.2 percent
for women and 4.5 percent for men—than were those who lived
alone or with others to whom they were not related—37 percent
for women and 28 percent for men. Among elderly families, poverty rates in 1999 were lowest among married-couple families
(4.0%), among those headed by four-year college graduates (2.6%),
and among white, non-Hispanics (3.6%) (table 2.2). Elderly members of race/ethnic minority groups were 4 to 5 times as likely to
be poor as were white, non-Hispanic families. Somewhat surprisingly, the rates of poverty among elderly families were lowest
among those 80 and older.

Elderly individuals living on their own in 1999 were far more
likely to be poor than were those living in families. Nearly 20 percent of those elderly individuals had incomes below the poverty
line in 1999, and elderly women (21%) living on their own were
at greatest risk of poverty. The unique poverty problems of elderly
women living alone have been highlighted in earlier studies of
poverty among the aged.[10] Among these elderly individuals living
on their own, poverty rates are quite high among those lacking high
school diplomas (32%), most race-ethnic minorities (42–45%),
and those born abroad (26%) or in Puerto Rico or one of the other
outlying territories of the United States (55%). With the exception
of the Senior Community Service Employment Program financed
under the Older Americans Act, neither the national government
nor state and local governments have funded workforce develop-

Table 2.2. Poverty Rates of Elderly Families in the United States by Family Type and Selected Characteristics of the Family Householder, 1999

Family Characteristic	Poverty Rate
All	5.2%
Family type	
Married couple	4.0
Male householder, no spouse present	9.8
Female householder, no spouse present	10.6
Age of householder	
65–69	5.5
70–74	5.5
75–79	4.8
80+	4.6
Educational attainment of householder	
<12 years, no diploma or GED	10.5
12 years, diploma or GED	3.3
13–15 years	2.9
Bachelor's degree or higher	2.6
Race-ethnic origin of householder	
American Indian	18.9
Asian	14.2
Black, not Hispanic	14.0
Hispanic	12.3
White, not Hispanic	3.6
Nativity status	
Native born	4.6
Foreign born	11.3

Source: March 2000 Current Population Survey public use files, tabulations by Center for Labor Market Studies.

ment programs to meet the needs of the nation's elderly poor. During Program Year 1998, only 530 individuals ages 65 and older received services under programs of the Job Training Partnership Act (JTPA) for economically disadvantaged adults—well under 1 percent of the total—and only 4,700 participated in a JTPA program for older workers.

All of the above estimates of poverty rates among the nation's elderly families and population were static, cross-sectional measures for given years. In the past decade, poverty researchers have paid growing attention to the dynamics of poverty, including movements into and out of poverty over time. Such research allows an examination of the persistence of poverty problems among various population groups over time. Annual exit rates from poverty by families and persons during the 1960s, 1980s, and 1990s reveal that the elderly are the least likely to exit from the ranks of the poor. For example, an analysis by the Council of Economic Advisers of exit rates from poverty between 1962 and 1963 found that only 20 percent of poor elderly families were able to exit out of poverty versus 45–50 percent of families with a head between 25 and 44 years of age.[11] Findings from the Survey of Income and Program Participation (SIPP) on annual exit rates of poor persons for the late 1980s and early 1990s yielded similar patterns by age group.[12] Only 15 percent of all poor persons age 65 and older in 1992 were able to escape from poverty during the following year, while 26 percent of all adults ages 18–64 were able to do so. The intensity of poverty problems among the elderly poor is also greater than that of their younger counterparts. Among those elderly who were poor for at least two months during 1993, they were 50 percent more likely than were those 18–64 to have been poor all 24 months during 1992 and 1993.[13] Poverty becomes a condition that, once engaged, is likely to besiege the elderly poor over their remaining life span.

Poverty Problems of Race-Ethnic Groups

The share of the resident population accounted for by members of race-ethnic minority groups has been rising since the late 1960s, fueled by the growth and changing national origins of foreign immigrants, whose ranks have included many Hispanics and Asians.[14] Between March 1974 and November 2000, the share of the national population represented by white, non-Hispanics declined from 82 percent to 71 percent, and this share will drop further when the 2000 Census population numbers are built into the official population estimates of the country. Preliminary findings of the 2000 Census revealed a larger Hispanic and Asian population than was previously estimated.[15] Both Hispanics and Asians have substantially increased their share of the U.S. population since the early 1970s. In 1974, less than 7 percent of the U.S. population was Asian or Hispanic; by November 2000, together they represented 16 percent of the nation's resident population. The findings of the 2000 Census also indicate that the number of Hispanics in the population (35.3 million) came close to matching the number of blacks (36.4 million), including those blacks who identified more than one race on the census form.

Interpreting the poverty statistics for persons and families in various race-ethnic groups is somewhat complicated by the fact that the immigrant share of the population in these various groups varies considerably, and immigrants typically face higher poverty rates than do their native-born counterparts. In March 2000, slightly more than 13 percent of the householders in the nation's families were foreign born; however, the foreign-born share of family householders ranged from lows of 0 percent for American Indians, 5 percent for white, non-Hispanics, and 7 percent for black, non-Hispanics to highs of 60 percent for Hispanics and 81 percent for Asians and Pacific Islanders. The poverty problems of immigrants are discussed more fully in the following section of this chapter. Poverty rates of members of race-ethnic groups continue to vary quite considerably, and the relative incidence of these poverty problems has changed somewhat over the past decade. At the time of the declaration of the War on Poverty, the poverty problems of black Americans received considerable attention from poverty researchers and policymakers. Over one-half of the black population was classified as poor in 1959 versus only 18 percent of the white population. Since then, poverty rates among blacks have fallen considerably, particularly during the economic boom years from 1993 to 2000, when the poverty rate of blacks declined by one-third from 33 percent to 22 percent. Blacks still remain 3 times as likely as white, non-Hispanics to be poor.[16]

As a consequence of their growing numbers and their relatively high incidence of poverty (21.2% in 2000), the share of the poverty population that is Hispanic has increased.[17] In 1987, Hispanics represented only 17 percent of the poor; however, by 2000, their share of the poor had increased to 23 percent. Over the 1990s the Asian population has been characterized by poverty rates that were 3 to 6 percentage points above those of whites but considerably below those of blacks and Hispanics. Asian poverty rates have declined sharply in the last few years, falling to 10.7 percent in 1999, the lowest recorded poverty rate for Asians over the past 13 years (the years for which Asian poverty estimates have been available from the U.S. Census Bureau). Their poverty rate ticked up slightly to 10.8 percent in 2000. White, non-Hispanics continue to experience the lowest rates of poverty in the nation.[18] In 2000, fewer than 8 of every 100 white, non-Hispanics were poor; however, given their large numbers in the national population, whites still accounted for 46 percent of the nation's poor in that year. Blacks were 29.1 percent of the poor in 1987 and 25.4 percent in 2000. The patterns of poverty rates for families in race-ethnic groups closely mirror those for the general population. During 2000, family poverty rates ranged from a low of 5.3 percent for white, non-Hispanics to highs of 19–24 percent for blacks, Hispanics, and American Indians. Families in each race-ethnic group experienced steep declines in their poverty rates over the 1993–2000 period, with each group experiencing at least a 23 percent decline in their poverty rate over this seven-year period of sustained prosperity.

Poverty among the Foreign-born Population of the United States

During the past few decades, population growth in the United States has been markedly influenced by immigration from abroad. During March 2000, there were 11.6 million persons residing in the nation who had been born abroad and had migrated to the United States sometime between 1990 and March 2000.[19] They represented 45 percent of the estimated net increase in the nation's population between April 1990 and March 2000. Including the children born in the United States to immigrant women during the 1990s would raise this share to 70 percent. U.S. Census Bureau estimates of the nation's resident population after the 2000 Census, including estimates of the undercount, revealed a population of 281.4 million, nearly 7 million larger than the estimates of the nation's population before that census.[20] Greater than expected immigration flows had to be a key factor underlying this higher population level. As Steven Camorata noted in a recent study on national immigration developments for the Center for Immigration Studies, "Immigration has become the determinate factor in population growth."[21]

Debates over the effects of immigration on labor markets, wage and income inequality, the job opportunities and wages of native-born workers, the size of the welfare population, and the budgets of state and local governments intensify.[22] Yet little empirical work has focused on the magnitude or structure of the recent poverty problems of the immigrant population, especially those who arrived in the United States during the 1990s. We remedy this deficiency through analysis of the March 2000 Current Population Survey (CPS). In March 2000, there were more than 9 million families headed by a person who was foreign born,[23] representing 1 of every 8 families in the nation (table 2.3). The 1999 poverty rate among these immigrant families was just under 16 percent, nearly twice as high as that among families with a native-born householder. In the aggregate, poor immigrant families accounted for slightly more than 21 percent of all poor families in the nation.

Table 2.3. Poverty Status of Families in the United States by the Nativity Status of the Family Householder, 1999 (numbers in 1000s as of March 2000)

Nativity Status	No. of Families	No. Poor	Poverty Rate
Native born	62,993	5,259	8.3%
Foreign born	9,032	1,417	15.7
Arrived 1990 or later	2,488	565	22.7
Arrived 1980–89	2,808	472	16.8
Arrived before 1980	3,736	381	10.2

Source: March 2000 Current Population Survey public use files, tabulations by Center for Labor Market Studies.

The incidence of poverty problems among these immigrant families varied by the timing of the arrival of the householder in the United States. As expected, the more recent arrivals, being younger, having less work experience, and having less time to assimilate into U.S. labor markets, were characterized by higher poverty rates. Nearly 23 percent of immigrant families headed by an individual who arrived in the United States during the 1990s were poor versus 17 percent of those who migrated to the United States in the 1980s and only 10 percent of those who arrived before 1980.

The structure of family poverty rates among immigrant families in 1999 closely mirrored that of families with a native-born householder, though at consistently higher levels (table 2.4). Poverty rates among immigrant families are highest for the youngest families and fall fairly sharply with age until the 45- to 54-year-old group is reached. The educational attainment of immigrant householders is strongly associated with their poverty status, with families headed by individuals lacking a high school diploma being about twice as likely to be poor as their peers with a high school diploma and 4 times more likely to be poor than their counterparts with a bachelor's or more advanced academic degree. Again, this pattern is typical for the native born, but the poverty rates of the foreign born do not drop as rapidly as their education increases. Of course, the foreign born typically have English language literacy and numeracy proficiencies far below those of their native-born counterparts, with negative consequences for their wage and earnings prospects, especially among men.[24]

Similar to the findings for the native born, there were fairly large differences in the poverty rates of immigrant families from differ-

Table 2.4. Comparisons of the Structure of 1999 Poverty Rates among U.S. Families with Native-born and Foreign-born Householders

Characteristic of Householder	Poverty Rate	
	Native Born	*Foreign Born*
All	8.3%	15.7%
Age		
<25	28.9	31.3
25–34	13.0	20.8
35–44	7.8	14.8
45–54	4.9	11.8
55–64	6.7	12.3
65+	4.6	11.4
Educational attainment		
<12 years, no diploma	22.6	26.6
12 years, diploma or GED	9.9	14.1
13–15 years	6.0	11.6
16 years	1.9	6.3
17 or more years	1.0	5.6
Race/ethnic origin		
Asian	8.7	10.5
Black, not Hispanic	22.2	16.1
Hispanic	17.6	22.3
White, not Hispanic	5.4	8.3
Prior year's work status		
Worked 40+ weeks full-time	3.0	7.2
Did not work 40 weeks full-time	16.4	29.3

Source: March 2000 Current Population Survey public use files, tabulations by the Center for Labor Market Studies, Northeastern University.

ent race-ethnic groups. The poverty rates of immigrant families ranged from a low of 8 percent for those headed by white, non-Hispanics to a high of 22 percent for Hispanics. In each race-ethnic group, with the exception of blacks, immigrant families were more likely to be poor than were their native-born counterparts. However, black immigrant families (accounting for only 6 percent of all immigrant families) had a lower poverty rate than their native-born black counterparts (16% vs. 22%), probably because they had more education and came to the United States for reasons related to their educational preparation.[25] Finally, the poverty rates of immigrant families were strongly linked to the intensity of the work effort of the family head in the prior year. Among those immigrant families whose head worked 40 or more weeks full time during 1999, the poverty rate was only 7 percent versus a poverty rate of close to 30 percent for those immigrant families with less intensive work effort during the year. Still, full-time work left the immigrant population with approximately double the poverty rate of the native born having the same work intensity.

The immigrant population probably will play an even more important role in determining both the size and the composition of the nation's poverty population in the coming decade in the absence of any substantive change in national immigration policy. Under its middle series population projections, the U.S. Census Bureau has assumed an annual inflow of 1 million to 1.25 million new foreign immigrants over the 2000–2010 period, and most past projections have underestimated the true size of these inflows, including both legal and undocumented immigrants.[26] During the past few years, several employer groups have lobbied the U.S. Congress to increase the number of highly skilled immigrants allowed to enter the country under the H1-B temporary visa program,[27] and the newly elected president of Mexico, Vicente Fox, has been encouraging President Bush to allow a more open border between Mexico and the United States to enable more Mexican workers to obtain employment in the United States.[28] The impact of the 11 September 2001 terrorist attack on the loosening trends in U.S. immigration policies remains to be seen.

Household Living Arrangements of the Poor

During the past few decades, the household living arrangements and marital behavior of the nation's population have changed in substantive ways that have had important implications for the size and demographic composition of the nation's poor.[29] The marriage behavior of the adult population has changed in key respects, with a rise in age at first marriage and higher separation and divorce rates, which have altered the marital status of the population.[30] The fraction of the nation's males (15+) who are unmarried has risen from 30 percent in 1960 to 42 percent in 1998, while the share of women who were not married rose from 34 to 45 percent.[31] The decline in marriage among black women was even more substantial over this period, with the unmarried group increasing from 40 percent to 64 percent. The median age at first marriage for both men and women has risen by four to five years since 1959. In that year, one-half of the married women had wed by age 20, but by 1997 and 1998 age at first marriage had risen to 25.0 years, higher than at any time since 1890. Among men, median age at first marriage increased from 22.5 years in 1959 to 26.7 years in 1998, exceeding that of 1890 by 0.6 years. Steep declines in the real annual earnings of many young adult men with no postsecondary schooling since 1973 have reduced their ability to form independent households, to marry, and to provide financial support for their children.[32] More young males (under age 30) live at home with their parents or other relatives today than was true in 1960, 1970, or 1980.

Closely related to this phenomenon is the fact that the education of women is increasingly exceeding that of men. For instance, in 1976–77, 93 women received associate's degrees for every 100 men who did so. In 1999–2000, that was true for 151 women per 100 men. For bachelor's degrees, the ratios were 86 women per 100 men in the earlier year compared to 133 women per 100 men in the latter year. The comparable numbers for master's degrees were 89 per 100 and 138 per 100. Ph.D.s granted to men still outnumber Ph.D.s granted to women, but that gap is shrinking. These gender education gaps exist for whites, blacks, Hispanics, Asians, and American Indians, and the trend is stronger among those from backgrounds of lower income. Since undereducated men will inevitably be less attractive as marriage partners to these better-educated women, the influence on family living arrangements is certain to be potent.

The number of couples who choose to live together outside of marriage continues to rise, with the number of such couples estimated by the U.S. Census Bureau to have increased eightfold between 1970 and 1998.[33] The rise in the share of births taking place out of wedlock, especially among young women under 25, combined with the effects of increased divorce and separation rates has radically altered the family living arrangements of the nation's children.[34] In 1960, nearly 88 percent of all children under 18 lived with both parents; however, by 1998, the share of the nation's children living with two parents had declined to 68 percent. While 84 of every 100 children living with only one parent reside in a home with their mother, the number of children living only with their father has tripled since 1980 to more than 3.1 million in 1998. As already stressed, those children living in single-mother families are the most poverty-prone group in the United States today.

Among the more important demographic effects of the delays in age at first marriage, the increased numbers of divorced and separated adults, the sharp growth in the number of unmarried couples, and longer life expectancy among the aged, especially women, is the substantial rise in the number of persons who live outside of "families," either living alone or with others to whom they are not related. The number of such "unrelated individuals" has increased by a multiple of 4 since 1959, and their share of the nation's population nearly tripled over the same period, rising from 6 percent to 16 percent. That is significant because poverty rates of unrelated individuals have been substantially higher than those of persons living in families over the past 40 years, although the relative size of the differences in the poverty rates of these two groups narrowed considerably between 1967 and 1979, primarily as a result of improved real incomes among the nation's elderly population. At the end of the 1990s, the poverty rate among the nation's population of individuals living outside of families was 19.1 percent, nearly double the poverty rate of only 10.2 percent among persons living in families. Poverty rates for unrelated individuals in 1999 were especially devastating for younger people (43% for those 16–24) and for those with less education (44% for those who had not completed high school). As a consequence of their higher rates of population growth and the deterioration in their relative poverty rate in recent years, these unrelated individuals have come to account for a rising share of the nation's poor population in the 1990s. By 2000, nearly 27 of every 100 poor persons were living outside of families, a share more than twice as high as the 12.5 percent that prevailed at the end of the 1950s.

Knowledge of the demographic and socioeconomic characteristics of the poor living on their own (or with other unrelated individuals) is essential for effective antipoverty policymaking. Poverty rates among these unrelated individuals in both 1989 and 1999 varied quite considerably across gender, age, educational attainment, and race-ethnic subgroups. Women were 33–40 percent more likely than men to be poor, and poverty rates were sharply higher among those under 25 and over 55 than they were among prime-aged individuals (25–54). In 1999, the incidence of poverty problems among the nation's unrelated individuals ranged from 44 percent for those lacking a high school diploma or a GED certificate to lows of 4–8 percent for those holding a bachelor's or more advanced academic degree. The least educated members of this group have much lower employment rates, and many have experienced declining real wages because of a reduction in the demand for less-skilled workers and a rising supply of immigrants with limited education. Among these unrelated individuals, poverty rates have tended to be twice as high among blacks and Hispanics as among white, non-Hispanics. Future antipoverty efforts will need to address the varied problems faced by the poor living on their own, with job placement, educational, and training strategies for the young and those in their preretirement years (55–64) and strengthened income transfer programs for those in their retirement years.

3. The Changing Geography of Poverty

Poverty problems in the United States have varied in intensity across geographic areas of the nation (regions, states, central cities, suburbs, rural areas) since the beginnings of the war on poverty, and progress in combating poverty also has varied geographically over time. In his classic book, *The Other America*, Michael Harrington noted that "the millions who are poor in the United States tend to become increasingly invisible," partly because "poverty is often off the beaten track."[1] Poverty in the early 1960s, according to Harrington, was geographically concentrated in the depressed factory and mining towns of the Northeast and Midwest, along the agricultural back roads of the South and Appalachia, in the black-dominated slums of the nation's central cities, on skid rows, and among the elderly, who often were socially isolated. The problems of the poor in Appalachia were well documented first by Harry Caudill in *Night Comes to the Cumberlands* and then in a series of books and studies on the depressed economy of the Appalachian region, which received national attention from both the Kennedy and the Johnson administrations.[2] In its initial 1964 study of the problems of poverty in the United States, which was based on a poverty threshold of $3,000 per family, the Council of Economic Advisers estimated that 47 percent of all poor families in the United States in 1962 were living in the South and that 46 percent of poor families lived in rural farm and nonfarm areas.[3] In estimating the number of poor persons in the United States in 1959 with the 1964 poverty methodology described in chapter 5, the U.S. Census Bureau identified a poverty rate of 35.4 percent in the South, which was 2.1 times as high as that in the rest of the nation.

Progress in reducing poverty in the nation's four regions (Northeast, Midwest, South, West) and nine geographic divisions has varied quite considerably over the past four decades (table 3.1). During the 1960s, each of the four regions experienced steep declines

Table 3.1. Trends in Poverty Rates of Persons in the Four Major U.S. Regions, Selected Years, 1959–2000

	Poverty Rate			
Year	Northeast	Midwest	South	West
1959	—	—	35.4%	—
1969	8.6%	9.6%	17.9	10.4%
1979	10.4	9.7	15.0	10.0
1989	10.0	11.9	15.4	12.5
1993	13.3	13.4	17.1	15.6
1999	10.9	9.8	13.1	12.6
2000	10.3	9.5	12.5	11.9
Percentage of change				
1979–89	−0.4	+2.2	+0.4	+2.5
1989–99	+0.9	−2.1	−2.3	+0.1

Source: U.S. Census Bureau, Historical Poverty Tables, www.census.gov, January 2001.

Note: —, no separate 1959 poverty estimate for the region.

in their poverty rates, with the incidence of poverty problems in the South declining by nearly one-half from 35.4 percent to 17.9 percent, although the South still remained the most poverty-prone region. National progress in combating poverty during the 1970s was far more uneven, with gains in the early years (1970–73) being offset by increases in poverty during the recessionary years at mid-decade. The South was the only one of the four major regions to achieve any substantive decline in its poverty rate over the decade of the 1970s. The Northeast region actually experienced an increase in its poverty rate of nearly 2 percentage points over the decade.

The 1980s witnessed a substantial shift in the economic fortunes of the nation's regional economies, with the Northeast, the South Atlantic region, and parts of the Pacific economy achieving strong economic progress in raising real outputs and incomes, while much of the Midwest, Southwest, Rocky Mountain region, and other areas performed less well.[4] Within the Northeast, the poverty rate in the New England region went from 8.6 percent to 7.6 percent by the end of the 1980s. The 1989 poverty rate in the New England region was equal to only 57 percent of the national rate and was the lowest in the nation. During the 1980s, poverty rates rose in the Midwest and the West and were statistically unchanged in the South.

During the 1990s, regional economic fortunes once again shifted. Between 1989 and 1993, the poverty rates in each of the four major regions increased, with the size of these increases being largest in the Northeast and the West, the two areas most severely affected by the recessionary environment of the early 1990s.[5] Since 1993, poverty rates have declined significantly in all four regions, with the South and the Midwest experiencing the largest declines. Over the decade as a whole, poverty rates fell in the Midwest, South, and West and increased modestly in the Northeast. The much stronger gains in the median real incomes of households in the Midwest and South during the 1990s were key factors underlying their greater success in reducing poverty problems during the decade of the 1990s.[6] While the Northeast region substantially led the nation in household real income growth in the 1980s, it was the only one of the four regions that failed to recover its 1989 median real household income by 1999. The regions' experiences during the 1990s revealed quite clearly that progress in reducing poverty is only possible with a rising economic tide as measured by improvement in the real income of the average household or family.

Viewing regional poverty developments over the past 30 to 40 years, the most striking finding is the steep decline in poverty in the South. Over the 1959–2000 period, the South's poverty rate fell from 35 percent to 12 percent, a decline of 65 percent in relative terms. In 1959, the South's poverty rate was 2.1 times as high as that of the rest of the nation, yet by 2000 the South's poverty rate was only 1.1 times as high as that of the rest of the nation, and adjusting state poverty rates for differences in their cost of living would have improved the comparative position of the South even more. The U.S. Census Bureau estimated that by 1994 the poverty rates of the South and West had become statistically identical, and they remained in that same position through 2000.[7] Poverty rates in the South were protected to an unknown degree by the fact that, during the years that so many elderly were moving there for retirement, they were also being relieved from poverty by the strengthening of the Social Security system, as noted in chapter 2.

Clearly, progress has been made in reducing the problems of poverty in Appalachia and other rural areas of the South visited by then-President Clinton in his summer 1999 poverty tour, but the problems of rural poverty in some of these areas remain relatively intense (poverty rates of 30% or higher).[8] Interviews with residents one year after the president's tour revealed little expectation that the federal government would or could do anything about the remaining problems. As Evelyn Nieves noted in her *New York Times* stories on the residents of these poor communities, "The idea that anything big might happen to places that have been down longer than they were ever up has long faded. And so has the notion, if it ever existed, that the federal government is the answer to the empty downtowns, idle laborers and the dilapidated buildings all too common in these communities."[9]

Poverty Rates by Geographic Divisions in the 1980s and 1990s

The U.S. Census Bureau categorizes blocks of states into nine geographic divisions. The poverty rates of the resident populations of these nine geographic divisions at the end of the 1980s and 1990s are displayed in table 3.2. As noted above, the New England region's economy had performed quite strongly in the 1980s, achieving the highest gains in real output per capita, per capita incomes, and family incomes, which allowed it to reduce the incidence of poverty problems among its population over the decade. Over the 1988–89 period, the poverty rate of New England residents was only 7.5 percent, the lowest of the nine geographic divisions and the only division to achieve a single-digit poverty rate. Poverty rates of persons across these nine divisions ranged from a low of 7.5 percent in New England to highs of 18–19 percent in the West South Central and East South Central divisions (table 3.2).

During the 1990s, changes in poverty rates across the nine geographic divisions varied markedly. In the New England, Middle Atlantic, and Pacific divisions, poverty rates at the end of the 1990s were higher than at the end of the 1980s, while poverty rates in all other regions had declined, especially in the East South Central and West South Central divisions, where poverty rates declined by 27 and 16 percent, respectively (table 3.3). Differences in poverty rates among the nine geographic divisions narrowed substantially during the 1990s. At the end of the 1980s, the gap between the poverty rate of New England (the division with the lowest poverty rate) and those of the West and East South Central regions was 11–12 percentage points. By the end of the 1990s, the gap between the poverty rates of New England and these two Southern divisions had narrowed to only 4–5 percentage points.

Poverty Rates of Persons across States

At the end of the 1980s, poverty rates of persons varied widely across the 50 states and the District of Columbia, ranging from lows

Table 3.2. Poverty Rates of Persons in the Nine Geographic Divisions of the United States, Two-Year Moving Averages, 1988–89 to 1998–99

Rank	Region	Poverty Rate, 1988–89	Rank	Region	Poverty Rate, 1998–99
1	New England	7.5%	1	New England	9.6%
2	Middle Atlantic	11.0	2	East North Central	10.1
3	East North Central	11.8	3	West North Central	10.1
4	West North Central	12.3	4	South Atlantic	12.0
5	Pacific	12.3	5	Middle Atlantic	12.3
6	South Atlantic	12.9	6	Mountain	12.4
7	Mountain	13.3	7	Pacific	13.6
8	West South Central	18.4	8	East South Central	14.0
9	East South Central	19.2	9	West South Central	15.4

Source: U.S. Census Bureau, Historical Poverty Tables for States, www.census.gov, 2001, tabulation by Center for Labor Market Studies.

Note: The East South Central division consists of the states of Alabama, Kentucky, Mississippi, and Tennessee, while the West South Central division contains the states of Arkansas, Louisiana, Oklahoma, and Texas.

Table 3.3. Percentage of Change in the Poverty Rates of Persons by Geographic Division, 1988–89 to 1998–99

Rank	Region	Change
1	East South Central	−27.3%
2	West South Central	−16.3
3	East North Central	−14.5
4	West North Central	−14.5
5	South Atlantic	−6.9
6	Mountain	−6.7
7	Pacific	10.9
8	Middle Atlantic	12.3
9	New England	28.8

Source: U.S. Census Bureau Historical Poverty Tables for States, www.census.gov, 2001, tabulations by Center for Labor Market Studies.

of 3 percent in Connecticut and 7 percent in New Hampshire and New Jersey to highs of 21–24 percent in New Mexico, Louisiana, and Mississippi. The New England region dominated the list of states with low poverty rates at the end of the 1980s, with four of the six New England states falling among the bottom seven states. Of the 12 states with the highest poverty rates over the 1988–89 period, 11 were located in the South. Table 3.4 compares the states with the 10 lowest and the 10 highest poverty rates in 1988–89 and 1998–99, using two-year moving averages for greater statistical accuracy. During those years, the poverty rates of 22 states were reduced by 10 percent or more, while 15 states experienced an increase of 10 percent or more. The degree of involvement in the booming high-tech industries, the proportion of Hispanics among the population, and the in-migration of foreign immigrants were probably the primary factors in the changes in rank, with the first factor being positive and the last two factors being negative influences.

Southern and Midwestern states dominated the list of 10 states with the largest percentage of decline in the poverty rate, while New England and Middle Atlantic states accounted for 8 of the 10 states with the highest increases in the poverty rate over the decade (table 3.5).

Table 3.4. Rankings of States by Lowest and Highest Person Poverty Rates on Two-Year Moving Averages, 1988–89 and 1998–99

	1988–89			*1998–99*	
Rank	*State*	*Poverty Rate*	*Rank*	*State*	*Poverty Rate*
1	Connecticut	3.5%	1	Maryland	7.3%
2	New Hampshire	7.2	2	Utah	7.4
3	New Jersey	7.2	3	Indiana	8.1
4	Vermont	8.1	4	New Jersey	8.2
5	Wisconsin	8.1	5	Connecticut	8.3
6	Rhode Island	8.3	6	Iowa	8.3
7	Massachusetts	8.7	7	Virginia	8.4
8	Utah	9.0	8	Alaska	8.5
9	Washington	9.2	9	Wisconsin	8.7
10	Delaware	9.3	10	Colorado	8.8
41	South Carolina	16.3	41	California	14.6
42	District of Columbia	16.6	42	Arkansas	14.7
43	West Virginia	16.8	43	Alabama	14.8
44	Kentucky	16.9	44	Texas	15.1
45	Texas	17.6	45	New York	15.4
46	Tennessee	18.2	46	Montana	16.1
47	Alabama	19.1	47	West Virginia	16.8
48	Arkansas	20.0	48	Mississippi	16.9
49	New Mexico	21.3	49	District of Columbia	18.6
50	Louisiana	23.1	50	Louisiana	19.2
51	Mississippi	24.6	51	New Mexico	20.6

Table 3.5. Ten States with Largest Declines and 10 States with Largest Increases in Two-Year Moving Averages of Poverty Rates, 1988–89 to 1998–99

State	Decline	State	Increase
South Dakota	−32.5%	Connecticut	140.6%
Indiana	−32.4	Rhode Island	30.3
Mississippi	−31.5	Oregon	27.8
Tennessee	−30.5	Vermont	21.7
Colorado	−28.9	New Hampshire	21.5
Arkansas	−26.3	New York	18.5
Kentucky	−24.0	North Dakota	18.1
Minnesota	−23.2	Massachusetts	17.9
Virginia	−23.0	Kansas	15.3
Maryland	−22.9	New Jersey	13.9

The determining factor, of course, was upward or downward trends in the median real incomes of households and the share of the total income pie obtained by families in the bottom quintile of the income distribution. States could remain among those with the lowest income and highest poverty rates despite substantial percentage changes in their poverty rates. The overall degree of inequality in state poverty rates declined during the years of high labor demand in the latter 1990s, reversing a trend of rising inequality during the 1980s. After the recovery from the 1981–82 recession, state poverty rates diverged, only to converge even more aggressively during the 1990s.

Interstate Differences in Cost of Living and Poverty Thresholds Adjusted for the Cost of Living

A major geographic issue in relation to the existing poverty income thresholds of the federal government is their failure to adjust the family poverty thresholds for differences in local, state, or regional cost of living. The poverty line for a family of a given size and age composition is the same in all areas of the country. In the early years of the national antipoverty effort, poverty thresholds were established separately for farm and nonfarm families in recognition of the fact that rural people were likely to be able to produce some of their own foodstuffs, as well as having access to lower-cost housing.[10] That differentiation was subsequently dropped at the end of the 1970s. However, many poverty analysts argue that living costs differ substantially not only on the basis of rural and urban living but also across metropolitan areas and states. Numerous studies of the cost of living in various metropolitan and non-metropolitan areas across the nation over the past two decades have revealed fairly substantial differences in the cost of living, with housing cost differences accounting for the bulk of the estimated differentials.[11] Failure to adjust existing poverty income thresholds for local cost-of-living differences, thus, distorts estimates of state and local poverty rates and can lead to a misallocation of scarce federal dollars for antipoverty efforts. Recognizing this need, the Committee on National Statistics of the National Research Council was assigned to study this issue, among others, in a review for Congress of the adequacy of the official poverty concepts and measures, assembling a Panel on Poverty and Family Assistance for the purpose.

The panel chose to use rental housing costs as its primary indicator of regional differences in the cost of living for the poor, using the national average as an index of 100 for purposes of comparison. Using data from the 1990 Census, that study found cost-of-living indices to vary substantially across states, ranging from lows of 84 in Mississippi and 86 in North and South Dakota to highs of 115 in California, 117 in Massachusetts, 120 in New Jersey, and 124 in Hawaii. Typically, the values of these cost-of-living indices were lowest in the South and the Midwest and highest in the Northeast and Pacific regions.[12]

These states' cost-of-living indices were then used to adjust the existing poverty income thresholds for families in each state, and a new set of family poverty estimates was generated. The use of cost of living–adjusted poverty lines leads to important changes in family poverty estimates and rankings for individual states. States in the Northeast and Pacific regions typically experienced increases in their poverty rates, which lowered their rankings, while many (though not all) states in the South and Midwest farm belt were assigned lower poverty rates (table 3.6). For example, while Connecticut and New Hampshire ranked fifth and ninth lowest in the family poverty distribution before cost-of-living adjustments, neither ranked among the ten states with lowest poverty in 1999, after cost-of-living adjustment factors were taken into account. While southern states dominated the list of the 10 states with the highest family poverty rates in 1999 using official poverty estimates, they accounted for only 5 of the top 10 states after cost-of-living adjustments. The northeast states of Massachusetts and New York and the Pacific region states of California and Hawaii were among the 10 states with the highest poverty

Table 3.6. States with the 10 Highest and 10 Lowest Family Poverty Rates before and after Cost-of-Living Adjustments, 1999

Before Cost-of-Living Adjustment	Poverty Rate	After Cost-of-Living Adjustment	Poverty Rate
	Lowest		
Maryland	4.4%	South Dakota	4.2%
Indiana	4.4	Indiana	4.2
Alaska	4.7	Maryland	4.4
Utah	4.9	Iowa	4.7
Connecticut	5.3	Utah	4.7
Minnesota	5.4	Minnesota	5.1
Wisconsin	5.4	Wisconsin	5.4
Virginia	5.6	Virginia	5.6
New Hampshire	5.8	Alaska	5.8
Iowa	5.9	Colorado	5.9
Colorado	5.9		
Average, bottom 11 states	5.2	Average, bottom 10 states	5.0
	Highest		
Kentucky	11.1%	Mississippi	11.1%
Arkansas	11.7	North Carolina	11.1
New York	12.1	Massachusetts	11.2
West Virginia	12.2	Texas	11.5
Alabama	12.2	Louisiana	13.7
Texas	12.4	New York	13.9
Mississippi	13.0	California	14.2
District of Columbia	15.1	New Mexico	14.4
Louisiana	15.2	Hawaii	15.4
New Mexico	15.3	District of Columbia	17.1
Average, top 10 states	13.0	Average, top 10 states	13.4

rates in 1999 when cost-of-living adjustments were made to poverty thresholds.

Trends in Poverty Rates within Metropolitan and Nonmetropolitan Areas, Central Cities, and Suburbs

As the problems of poverty were rediscovered in the early 1960s, much initial attention was paid to the problems of the rural poor, especially those residing in the multistate Appalachian region. The Appalachian region was singled out for several economic development initiatives under the Kennedy and Johnson administrations in the early to mid-1960s.[13] High fractions of the nation's poor were estimated to be living in rural areas, both farm and nonfarm, in the late 1950s and early 1960s. As the decade wore on, however, a combination of forces, including the Civil Rights revolution and the urban riots of 1964 to 1968, shifted the focus of national antipoverty efforts to the nation's large cities, especially the inner city or ghetto poor.[14] During the 1980s, new concerns arose about the plight of the poor in neighborhoods of concentrated poverty, and debates over the size and causes of an urban underclass took hold.[15] The original distinction between the urban and rural poor has been recast in recent decades as the annual poverty statistics of the federal government have focused upon the poor in metropolitan areas, including the central cities of those areas and their suburbs, and nonmetropolitan areas, many of which have experienced a demographic and economic renaissance in the past two decades.[16] These nonmetropolitan areas include both small cities (urban places) and rural areas, some of which have become gated communities for the affluent.

Over the past 40 years, the geographic structure of poverty rates for metropolitan and nonmetropolitan areas has changed substantially, although the bulk of these changes had run their course by the end of the 1970s. In 1959, nearly one-third of the residents of the nation's nonmetropolitan areas were estimated to be poor, twice the incidence found among the nation's metropolitan population (table 3.7). By 1973, the poverty rate of residents of nonmetropolitan areas was reduced by nearly 60 percent, and the relative size of the gap between the poverty rates of nonmetropolitan and metropolitan areas had declined to a multiple of 1.44. This ratio would fall further to 1.29 by 1979 and essentially remain there since then. While residents of these nonmetropolitan areas also faced poverty rates considerably above those of central city residents in 1959, they achieved parity by 1973 and improved their comparative position further by the end of the 1970s. Again, the relative sizes of the differences between the poverty rates of nonmetropolitan areas and central cities have remained stable since 1979, fluctuating between 0.87 and 0.88 in 1979, 1989, and 1999.

Within the nation's metropolitan areas, the poverty rates of both central city residents and those outside the central city declined steeply during the 1960s. By 1969, the poverty rate of central city residents had fallen to 12.7 percent, the historical low. Rates of poverty decline, however, were larger in the suburban portions of metropolitan areas over this period. As a consequence, the relative size of the differences in poverty rates between the central cities and suburbs increased fairly steadily through 1973, when a multiple of approximately 2.2 was reached. Relative poverty rates

Table 3.7. Trends in Poverty Rates of Persons, by U.S. Metropolitan and Nonmetropolitan Residence, Selected Years, 1959–1999

Poverty Rate (%)

Year	Metropolitan Area	Central City	Not in Central City (Suburb)	Nonmetropolitan Area
1959	15.3%	18.3%	12.2%	33.2%
1969	9.5	12.7	6.8	17.9
1973	9.7	14.0	6.4	14.0
1979	10.7	15.7	7.2	13.8
1982	13.7	19.9	9.3	17.8
1989	12.0	18.1	8.0	15.7
1991	13.7	20.2	9.6	16.1
1992	14.2	20.9	9.9	16.9
1995	13.4	20.6	9.1	15.6
1997	12.6	18.8	9.0	15.9
1999	11.2	16.4	8.3	14.3

Source: U.S. Census Bureau, Historical Poverty Statistics, www.census.gov.

of central city residents have remained roughly constant since then, with the exception of 1999, when the multiple fell below 2.0 for the first time since 1991, undoubtedly because of the high demand for labor that year.

The nature and character of poverty problems also vary between central cities and suburbs. The larger central cities, especially in the Middle Atlantic and Midwest regions, tend to have far more concentrated poverty problems (neighborhoods with poverty rates of 40% or more) than their suburban counterparts, and a much higher proportion of the poor in central cities are black or Hispanic. During 1999, two-thirds of all poor residents of the nation's central cities were either black or Hispanic, while only 43 percent of the poor in suburban communities were either black or Hispanic. In the nation's nonmetropolitan areas, a substantial majority of the poor (77%) in 1999 were white.

During the closing year of the 1990s, the incidence of poverty problems declined sharply in the nation's central cities, falling from 18.5 percent to 16.4 percent, yielding a poverty rate in 1999 that was nearly one-fourth below that of 1993. The U.S. Census Bureau estimated that nearly 80 percent of the net decrease in the number of poor persons across the entire country took place in the nation's central cities.[17] Despite these important gains, nearly one of every six residents of the nation's central cities were still classified as poor at the end of the 1990s, a poverty rate twice as high as that of the cities and towns making up the balance of metropolitan areas.

Some demographic analysts, including Harold Hodgkinson, have claimed that the nation's inner suburbs and some of its outlying suburban communities are beginning to compose a larger share of the poor in metropolitan areas.[18] Findings for all metropolitan areas combined in the 1990s seem to bear this out.[19] Between 1989 and 1999, the total number of poor persons residing in central cities declined from 13.6 million to 13.1 million, while the number of poor residents in the remaining portions of these metropolitan areas rose from 9.3 million to 11.7 million, an increase of 2.4 million. By 1999, the metropolitan poor living outside the central cities accounted for 47 percent of the poor population in metropolitan areas, up from 40 percent in 1989. The relative size of the difference in poverty rates between central cities and the suburban portions of metropolitan areas fell from nearly 2.3 in 1989 to slightly below 2.0 in 1999, reversing the situation that prevailed in the 1980s.[20]

**Problems of Concentrated Urban Poverty
and the Urban Underclass**

In the mid-1980s, poverty researchers began to pay increased attention to the problems of the poor in neighborhoods of concentrated poverty, to ghetto poverty, and to the growth of an urban underclass.[21] William Julius Wilson and other poverty researchers, including Christopher Jencks, John Kasarda, Mary Jo Bane, Paul Jargowsky, and Paul Peterson, examined problems of poverty in central city neighborhoods in which 40 percent or more of the residents were poor.[22] Research findings on the growth of such concentrated urban poverty by Bane and Jargowsky for the decade of the 1970s revealed that the bulk of the increase in "ghetto poverty" (inner city areas with poverty rates of 40% or higher) took place in the industrial Northeast and the Midwest. Ten central cities (eight of which were in the Midwest or Northeast) alone were responsible for 75 percent of the national increase in ghetto poverty during the decade of the 1970s.[23]

Jargowsky's updated findings for the 1980s revealed a continuation of growth of concentrated poverty in many metropolitan areas, although the magnitude of these increases varied across both regions, metropolitan areas, and cities.[24] In all metropolitan areas of the nation, the number of persons living in high-poverty census tracts (those with a poverty rate of 40% or more) increased from 2.381 million to 3.745 million between 1980 and 1990, an increase of 57 percent versus an increase of only 26 percent between 1970 and 1980.[25] The number of high-poverty census tracts increased in all nine geographic divisions during the 1980s; however, the rates of increase were substantially higher in both Midwest divisions, the West South Central, and the Rocky Mountain division than they were in the New England or Middle Atlantic divisions. While only 18 percent of all poor persons residing in metropolitan areas lived in a high-poverty neighborhood in 1990, poor blacks (33%) and Hispanics (22%) were considerably more likely than whites (6%) to be housed in a high-poverty urban neighborhood.[26]

William Julius Wilson has claimed that the existence of high levels of joblessness among adults in urban neighborhoods of concentrated poverty should be of greater concern to public policymakers than poverty itself. In his 1996–97 article in *Political Science Quarterly,* "When Work Disappears," Wilson argued that "the consequences of high neighborhood joblessness are more devastating than those of high neighborhood poverty. A neighborhood in which people are poor but employed is different from a neighborhood in which people are poor and jobless."[27] These high levels of joblessness in turn have been viewed by Wilson and some other social scientists as the primary economic problem prevailing in high-poverty neighborhoods and the underlying cause of the poverty, dependency, alienation, social disorganization, and problems with family stability encountered by residents. Concerns over the problems of concentrated poverty during the past decade have led to renewed research on the effects of neighborhood economic and social conditions on the schooling, labor market, and childbearing behavior of young adults and the changing geographic structure and concentration of poverty problems.[28] Ethnographic studies of the daily lives of youth and adults in these inner city poverty neighborhoods and in declining white, working class areas have allowed further insights on their labor market and schooling behaviors, daily life experiences, and outlook on life.[29] Several of these studies have revealed the fatalism of some teens in these neighborhoods, including those connected to the drug trade.[30] In recent years, the U.S. Department of Housing and Urban Development and the U.S. Department of Labor have funded new initiatives aimed at improving the economic base of and providing additional educational, employment, and training opportunities for youth residing in these high-poverty urban neighborhoods.

4. The Causes of Poverty

Why does poverty so persistently plague a substantial number of individuals and households in the wealthiest nation in the world? That question can be divided into two parts: What is it that determines *how many* are poor in any society? And, given that, what explains *who* are to be those poor? This chapter explores answers to both of those questions.

Why So Many Poor in the World's Richest Nation?

A comparison of poverty rates and income distribution between the United States and other relatively wealthy nations can provide insights into the first question. We in the United States have chosen to focus on the individual pursuit of wealth and to concern ourselves less with its general distribution. The implicit but unproven assumption is that a larger total gross national product and greater national power are the result of that less-equal distribution of income. Of course, it is possible that the same impetus that drives the front runners forward may also pull those at the rear to higher incomes than otherwise. However, in the United States, that relationship weakened considerably in the 1980s and the first half of the 1990s, though it appears to have recovered during the prosperous last half of the nineties. Comparison with some other nations, using comparable data, indicates that our inequality leaves those at the rear not only further behind in relative terms but with absolutely lower incomes than in some more equality-conscious nations.

The greater heterogeneity of the U.S. population might be cited as another factor in our high poverty rates, but that only raises the question of why incomes differ so widely by race and ethnicity in this country. Elimination of poverty—in terms of serious deprivation, at least—is a realistic policy choice for the United States, though one given serious attention only when a large enough component is poor and demands political attention, as in the 1930s. It is well to remember that we undertook our 1960s War on Poverty "on the cheap" at a time when cutting taxes remaining from World War II and the Korean War could spark enough economic growth to pay for the increased federal expenditures without anyone feeling the pain. Fighting poverty has never been as easy since.

The International Context

In seeking to understand the "why" of poverty in the United States, it is also important to consider our nation's income and wealth status among the nations of the world. The United States beyond any doubt has the greatest aggregate wealth and income in the world. It also has the world's highest per capita income when measured by purchasing power parity exchange rates, which take into account relative prices in different countries. Alternatively, Switzerland and the Scandinavian countries exceeded the U.S. per capita income in 1998 when measured by market foreign exchange rates. The United States has also led the world in productivity measures through most of the post–World War II period. Though U.S. productivity growth fell behind that of some nations for a time in the 1980s and early 1990s, it overcame that lag and led the world again in the late 1990s and into the twenty-first century. But the United States also has the most unequal income distribution system and the highest poverty level among all economically advanced countries (table 4.1).

The relatively high American poverty rates result from a less-equal income distribution, low earnings for the underprepared, a less-generous income support system, and a high proportion of single-parent families. A less-progressive tax structure and the general reluctance to fight poverty aggressively are also among the more apparent reasons for a high poverty rate. Despite the high median income of U.S. residents, low-income households here are worse off than in any developed country except the United Kingdom, which has a much lower median income. On the other hand, individuals with higher incomes are much better off in the United States than elsewhere. Cash or quasi-cash transfers (e.g., food stamps) and tax breaks were more effective in all countries in reducing the poverty rate among the elderly than in assisting families with children. The differences among the protections for the elderly in various countries demonstrate the potency of political organization in determining who gets help in many countries, including the United States (table 4.1).

The United States experiences less economic mobility out of poverty than do most other rich countries. Low-wage workers in the United States have been shown to remain in the low-wage la-

Table 4.1. International Poverty Rates, Various Available Years

Country	Year	Percentage in Poverty			Rank (highest poverty rate = 1)		
		Total	Elderly	Children	Total	Elderly	Children
United States	1994	19.1%	19.6%	24.9%	1	3	1
Japan	1992	11.8	18.4	12.2	4	4	7
West Germany	1989	7.6	7.5	8.6	8	10	9
France	1984	7.5	4.8	7.4	9	15	11
Italy	1991	6.5	4.4	10.5	14	16	8
United Kingdom	1991	14.6	23.9	18.5	2	1	2
Canada	1991	11.7	5.7	15.3	5	14	4
Australia	1989	12.9	21.6	15.4	3	2	3
Belgium	1992	5.5	11.9	4.4	16	8	15
Denmark	1992	7.5	11.3	5.1	9	10	13
Finland	1991	6.2	14.4	2.7	15	5	17
Ireland	1987	11.1	7.6	13.8	6	11	5
Netherlands	1991	6.7	4.1	8.3	11	17	10
Norway	1991	6.6	13.5	4.9	13	6	14
Spain	1990	10.4	11.4	12.8	7	9	6
Sweden	1992	6.7	6.4	3.0	11	13	16
Average excluding U.S.		9.8%	12.2%	11.3%			

Source: Mishel, Bernstein, and Schmitt, *The State of Working America, 2000–2001*, p. 393, as quoted from Timothy M. Smeeding, "Financial Poverty in Developed Countries: The Evidence from LIS," Luxembourg Income Study Working Paper 155, 1997. Poverty is measured as the share below 50% of median adjusted disposable personal income for individuals.

bor market five years longer than do workers in Germany, France, Italy, the United Kingdom, Denmark, Finland, and Sweden.[1] Poor households in the United States are also less likely to leave poverty from one year to the next than are poor households in Canada, Germany, the Netherlands, Sweden, and the United Kingdom (table 4.2). Given its relatively high levels of income and wealth compared to other advanced and democratic countries, one can only conclude that the United States has chosen its pattern of wealth and income distribution and its levels of poverty.

The Distribution of Income and Wealth

U.S. government poverty indicators have been based on money income rather than on wealth because the latter concept is more difficult to quantify. However, the distribution of wealth is considerably more inequitable in the United States than is the income distribution (table 4.3). The concept of net worth used in table 4.3 includes the sum of all of a family's assets—the value of its house, checking and savings account balances, stockholdings, retirement funds and other assets—minus the sum of all the family's liabilities—mortgage, credit card debt, student loans, and other debts. Although the less-prosperous and less-wealthy nine-tenths of the U.S. population earn nearly six-tenths of the total income, they have only three-tenths of the net worth and one-fifth of the total net financial assets.

Changes in real family income after World War II are displayed in table 4.4. The income share of the bottom 60 percent of the population has declined steadily, that of the fourth 20 percent fluctuated upward slightly for a time but returned to its earlier share by 1999, and only that of the top fifth—and especially of the top 5 percent—has risen.

Table 4.5 illustrates the same phenomena in terms of wealth rather than income. Over the last 40 years, the share of household net worth held by the wealthiest fifth has risen moderately, while the share of net worth held by the remaining 80 percent has consistently declined until the probably temporary blip during the last years of the 1990s. The top 1 percent of households had 33.4 percent of the country's total wealth in 1983 and 38.5 percent in 1995, before dropping slightly to 38.1 percent in 1998. With unemployment rates low during 1998–2000 and the recent stock market decline, that slight readjustment probably continued, with a reversal likely thereafter. Even among the top one-tenth of the wealthy, the proportions drop rapidly. The second 4 percent has only 56 percent as much net worth as the top 1 percent, the next 5 percent has

Table 4.2. Poverty Rates and Transitions into and out of Poverty (% of Population)

Country[a]	Average Poverty Rate[b]	Share Poor for Entire Period	Share Poor at Least Once over Period	Ave. Annual Exit Rate from Poverty (% of Poor)	Probability of Re-entry into Poverty after	
					1 yr	5 yr
Canada	11.4%	1.8%	28.1%	41.8%	16.0%	4.0%
W. Germany	10.2	1.8	19.9	37.0	17.0	7.0
Netherlands	6.1	0.8	12.1	43.7	na	na
Sweden	7.4	1.1	11.9	36.3	20.0	1.0
U. Kingdom	20.0	6.1	38.4	29.1	23.0	2.0
United States	14.2	4.6	26.0	28.6	18.0	8.0

Source: Mishel, Bernstein, and Schmitt, *State of Working America, 2000–2001*, p. 395.

[a]Periods covered: Canada, 1990–95; West Germany, Netherlands, Sweden, United Kingdom, 1991–96; and United States, 1988–93.

[b]Measured as percentage of individuals with less than 50% of median equivalent disposable income after taxes and transfers.

Table 4.3. Distribution of Income and Wealth in the United States, 1998

Wealth Class	Household Income	Net Worth	Net Financial Assets
All	100.0%	100.0%	100.0%
Top 1%	16.6	38.1	47.3
Next 9%	24.6	32.9	32.4
Remaining 90%	58.8	29.0	20.2

Source: Mishel, Bernstein, and Schmitt, *The State of Working America, 2000–2001*, p. 259.

Table 4.4. Shares of Total Income Going to Various Income Groups, 1947–1999

Year	Lowest Fifth	Second Fifth	Middle Fifth	Fourth Fifth	Top Fifth	First 15%	Top 5%
1947	5.0%	11.9%	17.0%	23.1%	43.0%	25.5%	17.5%
1967	5.4	12.2	17.5	23.5	41.4	25.0	16.4
1973	5.5	11.9	17.5	24.0	41.1	25.6	15.5
1979	5.4	11.6	17.5	24.1	41.4	26.1	15.3
1989	4.6	10.6	16.5	23.7	44.6	26.7	17.9
1999	4.3	9.9	15.6	23.0	47.2	26.9	20.3

Source: Mishel, Bernstein, and Schmitt, *The State of Working America, 2000–2001*.

only one-fifth the total wealth of the top 5 percent, and the second 10 percent has less than one-fifth the net worth of the first 10 percent. Of course, the bottom four-fifths of the population do considerably less well. The second fifth from the bottom had less than 1 percent of the total net worth and the bottom fifth, including the poverty population, were in the negative category as to assets. Few of the poor have any capacity to stave off poverty, even briefly, by converting assets into cash. The elderly poor, some of whom have paid off their home mortgages, may be in a better position, but only in recent years have innovative financing schemes permitted a few of the elderly to remain in their homes and simultaneously use this resource to ameliorate poverty. The stock market boom of the late 1990s is often cited as evidence of a widening holding of wealth. However, although 48 percent of U.S. households had stockholdings in 1998, most of them indirectly through retirement plans, the bottom 40 percent of households held only an average of $1,700

Table 4.5. Changes in the Distribution of Household Net Worth, 1962–1998

Wealth Class	Year						Percentage Point Change		
	1962	1983	1989	1992	1995	1998	1962–83	1983–89	1989–98
Top fifth	81.0%	81.3%	83.5%	83.8%	83.9%	83.4%	0.4%	2.2%	−0.1%
Top 1%	33.4	33.8	37.4	37.2	38.5	38.2	0.3	3.6	0.7
Next 4%	21.2	22.3	21.6	22.8	21.8	21.3	1.2	−0.8	−0.2
Next 5%	12.4	12.1	11.6	11.8	11.5	11.5	−0.2	−0.5	−0.1
Next 10%	14.0	13.1	13.0	12.0	12.1	12.5	−0.9	−0.1	−0.5
Bottom four-fifths	19.1	18.7	16.5	16.2	16.1	16.6	−0.4	−2.2	0.1
Fourth	13.4	12.6	12.3	11.5	11.4	11.9	−0.8	−0.3	−0.4
Middle	5.4	5.2	4.8	4.4	4.5	4.5	−0.2	−0.4	−0.3
Second	1.0	1.2	0.8	0.9	0.9	0.8	0.2	−0.3	−0.1
Lowest	−0.7	−0.3	−1.5	−0.5	−0.7	−0.6	0.4	−1.2	0.9

Source: Mishel, Bernstein, and Schmitt, *The State of Working America, 2000–2001*, p. 260.

worth of stocks. Households with incomes below $25,000 owned 3.7 percent of outstanding shares, compared to 72.8 percent for those with incomes above $100,000.

Inequality in income and wealth has persisted throughout recorded history. The reasons for inequality of income are many, some worthy and others unconscionable. The practical question ought to be what degree of inequality is necessary to maintain an adequate goad for productivity under the prevailing system. The operative question for public policy is what degree of inequality is politically acceptable at any point in time in a viable democracy. Inequality rose markedly in the United States during the 1980s and into the 1990s and then tended to stabilize during the marked prosperity of the last half of the 1990s. It remains to be seen whether the process of the rich getting richer and the poor getting relatively poorer will reaccelerate as the economy slows after 2001.

The "Who" of Poverty

As to what determines who gets to be poor, such explanations as the erosion of the traditional family, changes in the demand for unskilled or low-skilled labor, competition from low-wage foreign workers here and abroad, and absence of the skills and education necessary to obtain well-paying jobs are frequent answers to the question. But that still does not answer the "who" of those victimizations. There must be a more general classification of poverty's causes. If one examines those individuals and families who make up the population in poverty, the explanations of their status can be divided into four overlapping categories: the intergenerational, the natal, the situational, and the personal.

Many are born into poverty, reared in its environment, and find it difficult to escape. A very few are simply predestined to poverty by accidents of birth burdening them with physical or mental health disabilities that, unless they are born into families who can offer them lifetime support, will make it impossible for them ever to earn an above-poverty income.

Some in situational poverty choose to be there. A young couple may have left the homes of relatively prosperous parents to marry while continuing their educations to prepare themselves for successful careers. Their income may be below the poverty line for a few years, although they also may be receiving substantial material assistance from their parents. Their temporary status is of no concern to public policymakers. Others may have fallen into poverty because of a set of unanticipated happenings—a job loss due to an economic downturn, a bankruptcy, an illness, or a divorce, for instance. Most of those who were not poor or near poor before their situational difficulties arose will have a support group or other safety net upon which they can rely and will generally recover and move on. Those who lack that support group and do not have the means to return to substantial income within a reasonable time will probably stay in poverty and start a new intergenerational heritage.

In the past, many have been victimized into situational poverty by such factors as racial discrimination, but that force has lessened in U.S. labor markets. Others, starting from outside poverty, will make inappropriate lifestyle choices—becoming an alcoholic or a drug addict, becoming involved in criminal conduct, failing to obtain an education, or having an out-of-wedlock child and losing a support group in the process—and become immersed in poverty by often irreversible personal choice. Some of the first group will be in the last group as well, whether by choice or by inheritance.

Specific Causes of Poverty

Having demonstrated that the United States has chosen to accept more poverty than other developed countries and having cited intergenerational, natal, situational, and personal explanations for imposition of that poverty upon individuals and families, we can now explore specific causes within those general explanations. Those causes are generally found in the family and in the labor market. Since the inception of the War on Poverty, there have been contentious debates on the causes of poverty, including various analyses of the effects of family size, the changing structure of U.S. families, the human capital traits and labor market behavior of the poor, and the changing levels and distribution of wages for U.S. workers. The poverty problems of families with children, especially single-mother families, deserve special attention, given their increasing share of all poor families in recent decades. The chapter concludes with an analysis of the problems of the working poor and the labor market behavior of poor family heads in recent years.

Family Size and the Poverty Rates of Families

The long-term shift in the composition of the nation's families—especially the number and sex of parents—has prevented the overall poverty rate from declining to a new historical low in recent years. While family size has been a positive force in poverty reduction, the number and sex of parents has been a markedly negative factor. The size of families has an independent effect on the likelihood of their being poor for several different reasons. First, the official poverty income thresholds vary by the number of persons in the family and their age composition. The larger the family, the more people there are to feed, clothe, and house and the higher is the poverty income threshold. Second, the number and age distribution of children present in the home tend to influence the likelihood that adult women will be active participants in the labor market and the number of annual hours of labor that they will supply.[2] These relationships between the number of children and the labor force attachment of women tend to hold true for married women and for single mothers. The greater the number of children in the home, the less likely it is that the mother will work.[3] Thus, larger family size due to the presence of more related children under 18 years of age in the home can raise the expected incidence of poverty by reducing the annual earnings of the wife.[4] Husbands, in contrast, tend to supply more hours of work when there are young children in the home.[5] However, the positive effect of children upon the work hours of married men tends to be offset by the negative effects on wives' work hours.

Between 1964 and 1989, mean family size fell from 3.70 persons to 3.17 persons, a reduction of nearly 15 percent, and since it has fluctuated within a fairly narrow range (3.16 to 3.20). Most of the reduction in mean family size is accounted for by a decline of one-third in the average number of children, from 1.44 to 0.96. Only 52 percent of families currently include children, while those that do have an average of 1.9 children. The decline in the fertility of women in the United States since the mid-1960s has been attributed by some analysts to the rising costs of children, including the forgone earnings of mothers, while others cite a decline in the taste or desire for children in recent decades.[6]

The decline in mean family size in the United States through the late 1980s could have been expected to have a favorable influence on the overall poverty rate among families. In 1959, nearly 26 of every 100 families in the United States contained five or more members, and 6 of every 100 families had seven or more members. By 1989, however, only 14 of every 100 families had five or more members, and fewer than 2 of every 100 families had seven or more members, a 70 percent reduction. Over the same period, the share of the nation's families with only two members had risen from 32 percent to 42 percent, and it increased further to 44 percent by 1999. Families containing only two persons consistently have been characterized by the lowest poverty rates, with only 7.6 percent of such families being poor in 1999.

The presence of children in the home, especially children under age six, can be expected to influence the labor force behavior of mothers. Among wives in married-couple families, the share who were employed at some time during 1999 ranged from 76–79 percent among those with no or one child to 69 percent for those with three children and to a low of only 49 percent for those with five or more children. Among female family heads, the share with some paid work experience during the same year ranged from a high of nearly 86 percent among those with only one child to a low of 72 percent for those with four or more children. Mean annual hours worked by employed wives in married-couple families ranged from a high of 1,867 for those with no related children under 18 in the home to a low of 1,377 for those with four children. Among female family heads, mean annual hours of paid employment ranged from a high of 1,941 among those with no related children under 18 to a low of 1,430 for those with five or more children. The effect upon poverty rates is obvious. During 1999, the poverty rates of families varied from a low of 7.6 percent for families of only two persons to nearly 9 percent for families of four persons to 17 percent for families of six to a high of 30 percent among families of eight or more persons. If the size distribution of U.S. families in 1999 had been the same as that in 1959, the 1999 family poverty rate would have been 10.5 percent rather than the 9.3 percent rate estimated for that year.

The Effects of Family Structure

It is widely recognized that family poverty problems have become more concentrated over time among families with children and families headed by women. In 1959, there was relatively little difference in the poverty rates for families with and without children—20.3 percent compared to 15.9 percent. By 1991 the difference was nearly fourfold—17.7 percent for families with children and 4.8 percent for those without—dropping to threefold—13.8 percent to 4.4 percent—by 1999. As a result of the widening gap between poverty rates of families with and without children, the proportion of all poor families that consisted of families with children grew from 65 percent in 1959 to 80 percent in 1993 before declining back to 77 percent in 1999 and to 76 percent in 2000. In part, this reduction is due to the slower rate of growth of families with children—2.2 percent between 1993 and 1999 compared to an 8.4 percent growth rate for families without children. Another major factor is that families with children, including single-parent families, responded more strongly to the high labor market demand in the latter 1990s.

Of course, whether a household is a married-couple family or a single male- or female-headed family has a very strong independent effect on the probability that the family will be poor. Over the past 40 years, the share of the nation's households comprising married-couple families has steadily trended downward, reflecting increases in divorce and separation rates and a rise in the share of births taking place out of wedlock, thereby leading to an increase in never-married single-parent families. In 1959, slightly over 87 percent of all family households in the United States were married-couple families. Over the following 37 years, however, the share of families consisting of married couples declined steadily, falling to 86 percent by 1969, 82 percent by 1979, 79 percent by 1989, and slightly over 76 percent in 1996. The composition of families by family type continues to vary markedly by race and ethnic group. The share of families that were married couples in March 2000 ranged from a low of 48 percent among black families to 68 percent among Hispanic families to a high of 82 percent among white, non-Hispanic families. At the same time, the share of families headed by single men has doubled from 2.7 percent of all families to 5.6 percent, and the share of families headed by single women has risen from 10 percent to 17.6 percent.

Since 1996 there has been a modest rise in the married-couple share of families, with all of the increase taking place among black families. One contributing factor in this recent favorable development is probably the declining rate of births among the nation's teenagers in the 1990s, especially among black teens. The vast majority of these teen births had taken place out of wedlock and led to the formation of single-mother families.[7] A second factor, however, may be the increasing tendency for young single mothers of all races and ethnic groups to remain in the homes of their parents or other relatives rather than to form independent households, particularly in the wake of national welfare reform that places strict limits on the time that such single-parent families can rely on the benefits of Temporary Assistance to Needy Families (TANF) to support themselves and their children.

Poverty rates of families in the nation have varied considerably by family type over the past 40 years, with married-couple families consistently having the lowest rate of poverty. In 2000, family poverty rates ranged from a low of 4.7 percent among married-couple families to 11.5 percent among male householders with no

spouse present to a high of 24.7 percent among female householders with no husband present. When one or more related children
under 18 were present in the home, the poverty rate among female
householders rose to 32.5 percent. The growth in the number of
single-mother families combined with their high rates of poverty
have increased the share of the nation's poor families consisting of
women and their children, a process referred to as the feminization of poverty.[8] The poverty rates of families headed by female
householders consistently have exceeded those of married-couple
families by sixfold over the entire 1973–2000 period.

However, the 25 percent poverty rate among the nation's families headed by female householders in 1999 was the lowest recorded in the 40 years for which national poverty statistics are
available, having declined from highs of about 36 percent in each
of the recession recovery years of 1982 and 1991. The 32.5 percent
poverty rate among families headed by female householders with
one or more related children in the home in 2000 also was the lowest rate of poverty among such families over the past 40 years. Each
of these records was undoubtedly a result of the high labor market
demand of that year and of the effects of state and national welfare
reforms. Still, despite the progress achieved between 1993 and
2000, the poverty rate of female-headed families with children was
also nearly 6 times as high as that of married-couple families with
children in 2000. The proportion of all poor families that were
female-headed increased from 20 percent in 1959 to nearly 50 percent in 2000. Close to 50 percent of all black and Hispanic single-
mother families were poor in 1999, dropping closer to 40 percent
by 2000. In 2000, 6 out of 10 poor families with children were
female-headed, almost 3 times their proportionate share of all families with children.

Several characteristics of female-headed families make them
more poverty-prone than married-couple families. The most obvious is that married-couple families have a greater potential labor
supply than do female-headed families. In 1999, nearly three-
quarters of married-couple families had two working spouses, an
option not available to female-headed families. The necessities
of child care obviously make it difficult for the single mother to
work or to work full-time. Female-headed families also tend to be
headed by a younger householder with less work experience and
lower commensurate earnings potential.

In addition, the pathway to single-mother family formation has
changed over time, with more householders of female-headed families consisting of never-married women. In March 2000, 37 per-

cent of all families with related children headed by female house-holders consisted of never-married women, compared to 16 percent in 1980. More single-mother families today are started with an out-of-wedlock birth. These women are more likely to be young and to have truncated education and work experience due to childbirth. They also are less likely to marry and therefore are more likely to raise their children as single mothers and to experience extended periods of poverty and economic hardship. However, research on the long-term labor market consequences of adolescent motherhood has shown that, despite early motherhood, with no additional births, a stable marriage, and additional years of education and work experience, these young mothers can overcome the adversities that usually accompany early single motherhood.

The next most important factor is that the stock of educational capital in a female-headed family is typically lower than that in married-couple families. In March 2000, nearly 31 percent of the householders in married-couple families with children had completed at least a bachelor's degree, compared to only 12 percent of female householder family heads. An additional source of human capital and earnings in married-couple families is the spouse. Nearly 30 percent of the spouses in married-couple families had earned a bachelor's degree or more in 2000. At the lower end of the educational spectrum, householders in female-headed families were nearly twice as likely as heads of married-couple families to have failed to complete high school (23% vs. 12%).

Given the rising importance of education in determining earning capacity, it is inevitably difficult for such families to avoid poverty. During 1998, the poverty rates of married-couple families ranged from 16 percent among those families with a householder lacking a high school diploma or GED to slightly more than 1 percent where the household head had a bachelor's or higher degree. The poverty rate for female-headed families whose householder lacked a high school diploma or GED was just under 50 percent, compared to 7 percent when the female household head had a bachelor's degree. The education factor was also an important contributor to the high poverty rates of black and Hispanic female-headed families, whose average educational attainment was below that of non-Hispanic whites. If black families were distributed across family type and educational attainment in the same manner as whites, their poverty rate would have been 11 percent rather than 21.9 percent in 2000. The nearly 15-percentage point gap between the poverty rates of Hispanic and non-Hispanic whites would be reduced to 6 percentage points if Hispanics had the same family type and educational distribution as their non-Hispanic counterparts.

Future antipoverty efforts aimed at reducing racial and ethnic differences should focus on strengthening the educational attainment of those minorities and increasing their personal economic and social incentives to form and maintain married-couple families. Changes in federal income tax policies, including key provisions of the Earned Income Tax Credit (EITC) program, access to job training programs, and national health insurance and housing policies could help promote marriage among low-income adults in all race/ethnic groups. In too many instances, our social welfare policies and our antipoverty programs slight the needs of married-couple families and provide few incentives for low-income adults to marry.

The Cyclical Behavior of Poverty among Female-headed Families

The benefits of the economic expansion in the 1990s were more widespread than those of the expansions of the 1970s and 1980s, resulting in impressive reductions in the poverty rates among the more disadvantaged subgroups of families. A study of the 1947–68 period found that a 1 percent increase in median family income produced a 1.4 percent decrease in poverty.[9] Other studies of the statistical relationship between the poverty rate and the macro performance of the economy concluded that the relationship between the two variables weakened during the 1970s and 1980s but experienced a resurgence during the 1990s.[10] Between 1982 and 1989, the poverty rate of married-couple families declined by 26 percent, compared to a decline of only 12 percent in the poverty rate of female-headed families and of only 10 percent among female-headed families with children. The poverty rate of married-couple families headed by white, non-Hispanic householders showed a 34 percent reduction during the 1980s expansion, compared to 24 percent among black families and only 15 percent among Hispanic families.

The 1980s boom clearly benefited married-couple families more than female-headed families and white married-couple families more than their black and Hispanic counterparts. The 1990s expansion, in contrast, resulted in a decline of 20 percent in the poverty rate of married-couple families, compared to a 22 percent drop among female-headed families and a 24 percent decline among female-headed families with children. All three race and ethnic subgroups of female-headed families (white, black, and Hispanic) also made greater strides in reducing poverty during the

1990s compared to their experiences in the 1980s. The same was true among married-couple families headed by a black or Hispanic householder. However, white married-couple families did not fare as well in the 1990s as they did during the 1980s. Their poverty rate declined by 25 percent between 1991 and 2000 compared to a much larger relative decline of 34 percent between 1982 and 1989.

One of the reasons cited for the weaker link between economic growth and poverty during the 1970s and the 1980s was the decline in weekly real earnings experienced by workers at the bottom of the earnings distribution. These economic expansions lifted relatively smaller numbers of persons and families out of poverty and resulted in smaller reductions in the poverty rate. In the 1990s, the effects of welfare reform combined with an expansion of the EITC and an increase in the federal minimum wage to provide persons at the bottom of the economic ladder and persons coming off welfare rolls greater incentives to work. Full-employment labor market conditions and rising labor productivity also raised wages for less-skilled workers. An increase in the labor market attachment of these persons, an improvement in their earnings via the EITC, a higher minimum wage, and higher market wages are the likely underlying causes of the greater decline in the poverty rate during the 1990s, particularly among female-headed families with children under 18. Therefore, it is useful to examine more carefully the experience of female-headed families during the expansionary period that began in 1993 and appeared to be at least temporarily over by 2001.

Compared to 1993, there were 5 percent more families with related children under 18 in the year 2000. Over the same seven-year period, the number of female-headed families with one or more related children increased 6.1 percent. The proportion of all families with children that were headed by single women remained nearly constant, increasing only from 23.2 percent to 23.4 percent. The number of families with children headed by female householders and with incomes below the poverty line declined from 4,034,000 to 2,767,000 over that 1993–2000 period, a decline of 31 percent. As a consequence, the poverty rate of this group of families decreased from 46.2 percent in 1992 to 32.5 percent in 2000. The poverty rate of all families with one or more related children under 18 declined from 18.5 percent to 12.7 percent over the same period. Married-couple families with children had the lowest poverty rate of the three types of families and witnessed a decline in their poverty rate from 8.6 percent in 1992 to 6.0 percent in 2000. Therefore, although female-headed families with children experienced greater absolute reductions in their higher poverty proportions during these years, their relative gains were less than those of married-couple families.

There is a wide variation in the structure of poverty rates of female-headed families by their age, educational attainment, and race and ethnic origin. The largest declines in poverty rates occurred among families headed by younger and poorly educated householders. Among families headed by women under 25, the poverty rate declined by 20 percentage points, from 78 percent in 1992 to 58 percent in 1999 (table 4.6). Families headed by women 25–34 years old and those 45–54 years old both witnessed a decline of 10 percentage points in poverty rates during the same period. Although younger female-headed families continue to have higher poverty rates, the differences between the poverty rates across families by age of the female householder declined over these seven years. In 1992, the poverty rate of families headed by single women under 25 years old was more than 50 percentage points higher than that of their counterparts who were 45–54 years old (78% vs. 27.3%). In 1999, the difference between the poverty

Table 4.6. The Structure of Poverty Rates among U.S. Female-headed Families with Related Children under 18, 1992 and 1999

	Poverty Rate		
Characteristic of the Householder	*1992*	*1999*	*Change*
All	45.7%	35.7%	−10.0%
Age			
Under 25	78.0	58.0	−20.0
25–34	54.6	44.1	−10.5
35–44	35.8	26.9	−8.9
45–54	27.2	24.2	−3.0
Educational attainment			
Less than high school	70.3	60.0	−10.3
High school graduate	46.8	38.7	−8.1
Some college	32.7	24.1	−8.6
College graduate	11.4	9.6	−1.8
Race-ethnic origin			
White, non-Hispanic	35.4	25.4	−10.0
Black, non-Hispanic	57.0	45.9	−11.1
Hispanic	57.4	46.6	−10.8
Other, non-Hispanic	44.8	36.3	−8.5

Source: March Current Population Survey 1993 and 2000 Public Use Data Tapes, tabulations by the authors.

rates of these two types of families fell to 34 percentage points (58% among younger families vs. 24% among their older counterparts).

Poorly educated women gained the most ground in poverty reduction between 1992 and 1999. The incidence of poverty declined by 10 percentage points among women who failed to complete high school and by 8 percentage points among high school graduates and those female householders who had completed some college but had not earned a bachelor's degree. Among women householders with a bachelor's degree or more, the poverty rate declined from 11 percent in 1992 to 9.6 percent in 1999. Despite large declines, the poverty rate of poorly educated female householders remains substantially higher than that of their better-educated counterparts.

The poverty rate of female-headed families also declined across all race and ethnic groups between 1992 and 2000. The magnitude of the decline ranged from 12 percentage points among white families to 15 percentage points among black and Hispanic female-headed families with children. Nevertheless, in 2000, the poverty rate of female-headed families with children headed by a Hispanic or black householder remained 15 percentage points higher than the poverty rate of female-headed families headed by a white householder.

The major source of the decline in the poverty rate of female-headed families was the sizable increase in the employment rates among householders of these families. In 1999, the poverty rate among female-headed families with related children whose householder was employed for 1800 hours or more during the year was 12.6 percent compared to 67 percent among their counterparts who were not employed during the entire year. In fact the poverty rate of single female-headed families declined steadily as the work effort of the householder increased. If we restrict the sample of female-headed families with related children to only those families where the householder was under 55 years old, the differences in the poverty rate of nonworking householders and full-time year-round working householders is even greater.

Nearly 80 percent of nonworker female householders under 55 were poor while the poverty rate among women who were employed for 1,800 hours or more was 13 percent. However, a small amount of work effort did not help these families escape poverty. Those female heads of families who worked under 500 hours were as likely to be poor as their nonworking counterparts. Women working a small number of annual hours are employed intermittently during the year in low-wage jobs. The earnings from these jobs failed to lift the families of these women out of poverty. The poverty rate among women who worked between 500 and 1,000 hours annually was 68 percent or nearly 10 percentage points lower than nonworkers or intermittent workers and those who worked between 1,000 and 1,800 hours managed to cut down their poverty rates to 44 percent. The poverty rate of women who worked 1,800 hours or more (equivalent to a full-time year-round job) was only 13 percent. Although this poverty rate is much lower than that of other female-headed families, it reveals the unfortunate fact that despite full-time year-round employment in 1999 among heads of female-headed families, one out of eight remained poor. Because of low levels of skills, education, and work experience, many of these women secure low-wage jobs that do not lift them out of poverty, even when they work full-time throughout the year. Not just jobs but opportunities to increase earning capacity are essential to future poverty reduction among these women.

The amount of time available for employment is critical to the potential economic well-being of female-headed families. Between 1992 and 1998, the proportion of single female householders with children who were employed for at least one week during the year increased from 68 percent to 81 percent. This increase in employment of female householders occurred over the same time period as the nation's public assistance caseloads declined by 52 percent from 4,963,000 families in January 1993 to 2,358,000 families in December of 1999.[11]

Declines in public assistance caseloads were closely associated with an increase in the labor force attachment of single mother householders. Improvement in macroeconomic conditions, rewarding work with incentives in the form of the Earned Income Tax Credit and higher minimum wages, and time-limited welfare benefits all played an important role in increasing the labor market attachment of single mothers. However, poverty declined at a slower rate compared to the stunning increase in labor force attachment of these women. Studies have identified employment in low-wage and low-skills jobs, lack of transportation or dependable child care, and the inability to utilize available benefits after leaving welfare due to a lack of knowledge or fear as some of the reasons for this less than proportionate decline in poverty.[12]

Decrease in the receipt of public assistance income and increases in employment were particularly strong among young and poorly educated women. According to their responses to the Current Population Survey, in 1992, nearly two out of three young female householders (under 25) with one or more children under 18 received public assistance income during the year. The proportion declined to 28 percent in 1999. Over the same time period, the proportion of these young women who had worked at some point during the year increased from 57 percent to 80 percent. Among 25- to 34-year-olds, the proportion that received public assistance income was halved from 40 percent in 1992 to 19 percent in 1999 and the proportion who were employed at some time during the year increased from 70 percent in 1993 to 85 percent in 1999. There were declines in the receipt of public assistance incomes across all age groups of women. At the end of the 1990s, as was true at the beginning of the decade, younger women were more likely to receive public assistance income than were their older counterparts. The difference between age groups narrowed somewhat over this seven-year period.

Reliance on public assistance income and employment also varied by educational attainment. Single female householders with children who failed to complete high school were much more likely to receive public assistance than their better-educated counterparts. In 1999, one-third of high school dropouts received public assistance income compared to only 4 percent of female householders who had earned at least a bachelor's degree. Declines in the receipt of public assistance were also largest among poorly educated women. The incidence of receipt of public assistance income among high school dropouts declined from 55 percent in 1992 to 32 percent in 1999. Among high school graduates, the incidence declined from 33 percent to 15 percent and among women with some college but no bachelor's degree, the incidence declined from one-quarter to one in ten between 1992 and 1999.

The relationship between declines in public assistance receipt and increased work effort by single mothers underlies some of the declines in poverty rates of single female-headed families during the 1993–99 period. However, as noted earlier for all low-income women, increased work effort did not solve the poverty problem for many of these former welfare recipients. Even full-time and year-round employment in 1999 left one out of eight of these women with incomes below the poverty line. Many of these women lack the skills and education necessary to secure a well-paying job, so they end up poor despite high levels of work effort. Although full-time and year-round work lifts many female-headed families out of poverty, unfortunately, there are families whose poverty problems need more than a full-time and year-round job.

These women need an upgrading of their skills so that they can secure higher paying jobs and lift themselves out of poverty.

The Working Poor

The above findings concerning the employment of female family heads and former recipients of public assistance suggest the need for further analysis of the situations of those who continue in poverty despite their labor market participation. Defining the working poor is a task that is not as simple as it may seem. The recent literature on poverty contains a wide variety of such definitions, including the following from the U.S. Bureau of Labor Statistics: "The person who participates in the civilian labor force for 27 or more weeks during the year but lived in a family with a combined money income below the poverty line for a family of that size and age composition." That definition guides the following comments.

The working poor as a proportion of all of those in the civilian labor force for 27 or more weeks varied from 5.1 percent to 6.7 percent throughout the 1990s. During 1999, 42.6 percent of poor persons 16 years of age or older worked sometime during the year, 31.8 percent were in the labor force and either employed or unemployed, but only 11.7 percent worked full time for the full year.

Fifty-four percent of all poor family heads worked at some point during that year, the proportions varying considerably by age. Nearly two-thirds of those under age 45 were employed at some time during the year versus only 4 of every 10 poor family heads between the ages of 45 and 64 and only 1 of every 10 elderly family heads. The weak labor force attachment of these elderly, poor family heads is a prime factor contributing to their high persistence rates in poverty. For younger poor families, increased work and higher wages, especially during full-employment labor market conditions, enables more of them to escape from the ranks of the poor over time.

The ability of nonelderly families to escape poverty is strongly linked to the amount of their work effort during the year. During 1999, nearly three of every 10 nonelderly families whose householder did not work at all during the year were poor as were 29 of every 100 families whose householder worked fewer than 1,000 hours. Increased work effort over 1,000 hours was associated with much lower poverty rates, including a poverty rate of 16.2 percent for those working 1001–1800 hours a year and only 3.4 percent for nonelderly families with a householder who worked 1800 or more hours during the year. Adding in the value of EITC payments, food stamp, and rental subsidies received by the latter group of families would reduce their poverty rate even further.

Poor family heads employed at some time during 1999 worked an average of 37 weeks and 1372 hours, varying only modestly by age group for those 25 and older. The youngest of the poor family heads (those under 25) tend to work the least, being employed for an average of 32 weeks and 1127 hours during 1999. Those 45 to 64 years of age averaged 38 weeks and 1480 hours of work. The part-time employed continued to outnumber the full-time employed, as is to be expected among a population including so many single-parent families. Nevertheless, that 1372 hours in 1999 was up from 961 hours of work averaged by poor families in 1979. In 1979, more than one-third of poor family heads with children did not work at all but this had fallen to one-fourth twenty years later. The average hours worked by female-headed families increased from 515 in 1979 to 808 in 1999. In the former year, only 7.7 percent of single-mother families worked at least 2000 hours but that had doubled over the subsequent two decades. However, at an average wage of $6.45 a single parent with two children would have had to work 2,036 hours just to reach the poverty threshold of $13,133. Still, a surprisingly large percentage of nonelderly adults have full-time, full-year attachments to the labor force but have annual earnings sufficiently low to keep them in poverty in the absence of other family earnings or nonwage income—that is true of 17.5 percent of all workers, 13.1 percent of men and 23.7 percent of women. Considering both the employment rates of poor family heads and their work effort during 1999, only one of five poor, nonelderly family heads worked year-round, full-time (50 or more weeks of employment at 35 or more hours of work per week).[13] Of all nonelderly family householders who worked year-round, full-time during 1999, only 3.1 percent had incomes below the poverty line—1.9 percent if it was a married-couple family, which also benefits from the labor market earnings of their spouses and children.

While the number of poor persons in the prime working-age group, those aged 25 to 54, increased from 7,659,000 in 1979 to 11,108,000 in 1998, the percentage of the poor who were not employable rose from 17.6 percent to 26.5 percent, primarily because of illness or disability. Thus, those who were employable fell from 82.4 percent to 73.5 percent. But of the employable, the proportion unable to find jobs rose from 4.4 percent to 5.3 percent, despite the rising demands for labor.

The incidence of poverty problems among members of the nation's labor force in 1999 varied by gender, race-ethnic origin, and
educational attainment (figure 4.1). Women were modestly more
likely than men to be poor (5.9% vs. 4.4%), blacks and Hispanics
were approximately 2-1/2 times more likely to be poor than whites,
and those labor force participants lacking a high school diploma
were more than twice as likely to be poor as high school graduates
and 11 times more likely to be poor than workers with four or more
years of college, whose poverty rate was only 1.3 percent during
1999.

The Working Poor by Industry and Occupation

Wages and working conditions in the United States vary quite considerably by industry and by major occupation. For example, during 1999, the average weekly earnings of production or nonsuper-
visory workers on private nonfarm payrolls ranged from a low of
$263 in retail trade to a high of $746 in the nation's mining industries.[14] Across major occupational groups, the median weekly
earnings of full-time wage and salary workers ranged from highs
of $800 for professional workers and $792 for executives and man-
agers to lows of $363 for laborers, helpers, cleaners, $336 for service workers and $329 for sales clerks/cashiers, and vendors.
Given this substantial diversity in weekly wages and earnings by
major industry and occupation, it should come as no surprise to

**Fig. 4.1. Percentage of U.S. Labor Force Participants Who Were Poor dur-
ing 1999 by Gender, Race-Ethnicity, and Educational Attainment**

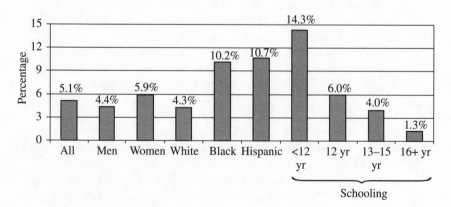

Source: U.S. Census Bureau, Current Population Reports

discover that both the working poor and low-wage workers in general are over-represented in certain major industries and occupations.[15]

During 1999, the poverty rates of families with a householder who worked 40 or more weeks during the year varied quite considerably by major industrial sector. Overall only 4.4 percent of such families were poor; however, their poverty rates ranged from lows of 1 percent or less in the mining and public administration sectors to highs of nearly 10 percent in retail trade, 11 percent in agriculture, forestry, and fishing, and 15 percent in personal services industries (cleaning, laundry, barbershops, private household industries). Very similar patterns prevailed in 1998, with workers experiencing much higher poverty rates in agriculture, retail trade, and personal service industries.

Family poverty rates of workers with substantive work experience also vary quite widely by major occupational category. Workers in professional, technical, and managerial occupations had family poverty rates of less than 1 percent in 1999 while workers in cashier and sales clerk positions, private household jobs, food and health services, and construction laborer positions had double-digit poverty rates in 1999. Future antipoverty strategies to reduce poverty among the working poor with substantive labor market attachment need to identify ways for increasing the productivity and wages of workers in those industries and occupations with a high incidence of working poor problems.

The Wage Factor

Trends in real wages and earnings, which constitute the lion's share of personal income for the typical nonelderly household, significantly influence the extent of poverty. Average real wages rose steadily from the end of the Second World War until 1973, then declined during the 1980s and into the 1990s, beginning a recovery in the mid-1990s that was being threatened at the turn of the millennium by rising unemployment. Table 4.7 displays trends in real hourly wages for workers at various points along the wage distribution between 1973 and 1999.

Only the top 20 percent of earners were able to improve their real wage levels from 1973 to 1995. All others experienced real wage declines during the 1979–95 period, though all experienced some recovery during 1995–99. The lower half experienced net wage declines for the entire 1973–99 period, with the lowest 10 percent suffering most greatly. Though paid less, only the lower 30

Table 4.7. Real Hourly Wages for All Workers by Wage Percentile, 1973–1999 (1999 Dollars)

Year	10	20	30	40	50	60	70	80	90	95
Real hourly wage										
1973	$6.30	$7.60	$9.04	$10.51	$12.05	$13.80	$16.05	$18.35	$23.06	$28.94
1979	6.67	7.61	8.93	10.51	11.89	13.78	16.29	18.99	23.31	28.28
1989	5.60	6.97	8.35	9.98	11.60	13.55	16.12	19.28	24.35	29.91
1995	5.53	6.76	8.08	9.51	11.07	13.10	15.62	18.91	24.43	30.64
1999	6.05	7.35	8.72	10.10	11.87	13.93	16.45	19.93	26.05	33.25
Percentage of change										
1973–79	5.8%	0.1%	−1.1%	0.0%	−1.3%	−0.3%	1.5%	3.5%	1.1%	−2.3%
1979–89	−16.1	−8.5	−6.5	−5.0	−2.4	−1.7	−1.0	1.5	4.5	5.7
1989–95	−1.1	−2.9	−3.3	−4.7	−4.6	−3.3	−3.1	−1.9	0.3	2.5
1995–99	9.3	8.8	7.9	6.2	7.3	6.4	5.3	5.4	6.6	8.5
1979–99	−9.3	−3.3	−2.4	−3.9	−0.2	1.1	1.0	4.9	11.7	17.6

Source: Mishel, Bernstein, and Schmitt, *The State of Working America, 2000–2001*, p. 124.

percent of employed women suffered wage losses during 1973–89 and only the bottom 20 percent—those most likely to have been in poverty already—suffered real wage losses for the entire 1973–99 period. As a result of these divergent wage trends, the gender wage gap declined persistently until women who on the average earned 63.1 percent of male wages in 1973 were earning at or above 75 percent of male wages during the 1990s. Applying the wage analysis more directly to the poverty level, the share of male workers receiving below poverty wages increased persistently from 13 percent in 1973 to 22 percent in 1995, declining thereafter to 20 percent in 1999, still well above the 1973 level. The share of working women receiving below-poverty wages declined from 40 percent in 1973 to 34 percent in 1999. Compensation is, of course, not limited to wages. The proportion of all workers with health insurance and pension coverage followed essentially the same path as real wages during the last two decades of the twentieth century, leaving about two-thirds with employer-provided health benefits and one-half earning pensions. But few workers in the poverty ranks were recipients of such benefits.

A major factor in the underlying real wage declines was the depreciating labor market worth of the undereducated and the rising wage premium for workers with higher education (table 4.8). Fortunately, the educational attainment of the employed labor force

Table 4.8. Changes in Real Hourly Wage by Education, 1973–1999 (1999 Dollars)

Year	<High School	High School	Some College	College Grad.	Adv. Degree
Hourly wage					
1973	$11.64	$13.34	$14.37	$19.46	$23.53
1979	11.58	12.99	13.89	18.21	22.24
1989	9.73	11.86	13.32	18.68	24.08
1995	8.57	11.33	12.57	18.80	24.80
1999	8.83	11.83	13.37	20.58	26.44
Share of employment					
1973	28.5%	38.3%	18.5%	10.1%	4.5%
1979	20.1	38.5	22.8	12.7	6.0
1989	13.7	36.9	26.0	15.6	7.9
1995	10.8	33.3	30.5	17.3	8.0
1999	10.8	32.3	29.6	18.6	8.6

Source: Mischel, Bernstein, and Schmitt, *The State of Working America, 2000–2001,* p. 156.

was rising, but that was not making it any easier for the undereducated to achieve rising real wages.

Educational deficiencies have been an increasing factor in explaining who is poor among families with children. Whereas the poverty rate for those family heads with less than a high school education was 19.4 percent in 1969, it was 39.1 percent in 1998. Similar comparisons for those two years were 6.6 percent to 17.7 percent for high school graduates and 5.4 percent to 10.3 percent for those with some college. However, the poverty rate for college graduates was 2.0 percent in 1969 and 2.3 percent in 1998.

A significant factor in explaining the wage decline of the less educated and the changing educational requirements of the workforce has been the shifting industrial structure of employment in the United States in recent years. Goods-producing jobs (manufacturing, mining, and construction), which averaged hourly pay of $21.86 in 1997, declined from 26.5 million jobs in 1979 to 25.5 million in 1999, having dipped even lower before the strong economic recovery after 1995. The greatest losses were in manufacturing where 2.5 million jobs—13.2 percent of the total—disappeared in those two decades. On the other hand, service producing jobs averaging only $16.73 an hour increased from 63.4 million to 103.3 million over that same period. Goods producing jobs had declined from 29.5 percent of total employment to 19.8 percent while service producing jobs had grown from 70.5 percent to 80.2 percent of total employment.

The accompanying decline in unionization from 24 percent to 14 percent of the workforce during the past 20 years had a considerable effect in reducing or restraining real wage growth, though it is difficult to estimate the influence on wages at the very bottom of the wage structure. The continuing decline in the real value of the federal minimum wage from a peak of $7.90 an hour in 1968 to $4.80 by 2000 (both in 2000 dollars) is a more clearly assignable factor in the continuance of poverty. Declining job stability in terms of reduced median years with the same employer and a declining share of employed workers in long-term jobs is also probably a factor in the persistence of poverty.

Employment Barriers of the Nonworking Poor

Nearly one-half of the nation's poor family heads reported no work at all during calendar year 1999, despite the low overall unemployment rate. Their impoverishment stems from an absence of any ties to the labor market. For those persons with no paid employment during the previous year, the March Current Population Survey (CPS) supplement captures information on their main reason for not working. Among all poor jobless family heads under 65, the three most frequently cited reasons for not working were taking care of home or family (44%), being ill or disabled (33%), and being retired (11%). Only 4.3 percent of the respondents cited the lack of available work as a major barrier to their employment, while 8.8 percent cited school attendance. The proportion of nonemployed poor family heads citing the nonavailability of work as their reason for not working fell steadily throughout the 1990s as the national unemployment rate declined.

The labor market barriers of the nonelderly poor, however, go well beyond the reasons that many cited for a failure to seek work. Many of the jobless adult poor lack adequate education and have severe literacy and numeracy deficits that restrict their employability and limit their earnings potential.[16] Attracting them into the labor market may require major investments in their human capital and wage subsidies to make work more attractive than the current labor market is willing to offer, even when supplemented with EITC payments. The number of nonelderly adults receiving Supplemental Security Income (SSI) disability and SSDI payments have increased markedly since the late 1980s, but until recently with the passage of the Ticket to Work and Employment Incentive Act of 2000, there have been few systematic ties between local workforce development systems and the SSI or SSDI programs. In the high labor demand of 1999, only 6.5 percent of poor, jobless family heads under 65 years of age indicated that they had looked for work, down from 14.0 percent in 1992, at the beginning of the recovery from the 1990–91 recession.

When they did look for work, the jobless poor cited an average of 26 to 27 weeks in each of three years spent looking for work. Many of the unemployed poor seem to suffer from severe structural problems, being unable to find any paid work in a full-employment labor market, though they constitute a small minority of the jobless poor family heads. A major challenge facing the nation's welfare to work and workforce development systems in the twenty-first century is to find new ways to attract these remaining poor jobless family heads into the paid labor force and to promote their employability and earnings once they enter the labor market. New, creative solutions will have to be found, building on the foundations of the Canadian Self-Sufficiency Program and the Minnesota Family Investment Program, both of which had moderate success in reducing poverty among longer-term welfare recipients by strengthening economic incentives to work. They are, however, no panacea to the poverty problems of the dependent poor in the United States.

Durations of Poverty and Exit Rates out of Poverty

The relative stability of the poverty rate over time masks considerable variability in individual poverty experiences and the movement of persons into and out of poverty. The most recent data concerning poverty duration seems to be that for 1994, but that data set is worth reviewing. There were 37.6 million poor Americans in an average month in 1993, a poverty rate of 14.6 percent. However, statistics from the U.S. Census Bureau Survey of Income and Program Participation show that 52.7 million people, or 20.8 percent of the population, were poor for two months or more during that year. There is substantial turnover in the poverty ranks. One in five persons who were poor in 1992 (21.6%) were not poor in 1993. The 6.3 million people leaving poverty were offset by 6.5 million who moved into poverty during the same period. Whites experienced significantly higher exit rates than did Hispanics, whose exit rates were higher than those of blacks. Individuals 18 to 64 years of age had a higher exit rate than either individuals under age 18 or over 64, and the rate for married-couple households exceeded that for all other household types. Finally, one in four (24%) poverty spells in the years 1992 to 1994 lasted more than twelve months, and 13 percent lasted more than two years. These findings suggest that a large segment of the American population is susceptible to at least temporary deprivation and that poverty is more pervasive than annual poverty rates indicate.

For most households, poverty is not a long-term affliction, but back and forth movement between poor and near poor is. Periods spent in school, accidents or poor health, job loss, family breakup, and other temporary factors may be involved for some—the situational factors referred to earlier in the chapter. Nearly one-half (46%) of poverty spells in 1992–94 lasted four months or less, and 67 percent lasted less than eight months—the most recent data available on the topic. However, persistent poverty plagues a substantial proportion of the poor. Twelve million, more than one-third of the 38 million poor in 1992, were poor for all twenty-four months of 1992 and 1993. One-fourth of all poverty spells last five or more years, and 12 percent last a decade or more. Lengthy periods of destitution for a minority of the poor translates into an average duration of approximately four years.

Whites and two-parent families are more likely to experience primarily transitory poverty, but blacks and children born into poor families more often experience long-term destitution. For example, if we use poverty in every month of 1992 and 1993 as a proxy for persistent poverty, 15.1 percent of blacks were persistently poor, compared with 10.3 percent of Hispanics and 3.1 percent of whites. Similarly, 17.2 percent of individuals in female-headed families were persistently poor, compared with only 1.6 percent in married-couple families and 8.1 percent among unrelated individuals. Nevertheless, though a few, such as those experiencing poverty while completing their education, leave poverty far behind thereafter, most of the entry and exit is by those whose marginal earnings result in their fluctuating just above and just below the poverty threshold and is therefore affected by the deterioration of the poverty standard alluded to in chapter 1 and explored more thoroughly in chapter 5. Well-off people may move temporarily into poverty due to a job dislocation, bankruptcy, or similar circumstance, then work their way back to prosperity. Their children may marry while in school and temporarily show poverty incomes. But most of them have support systems to assist their recovery. Some children from poor families obtain an education, develop strong literacy skills, and make an intergenerational transition to prosperity. Most of the poor move back and forth between the ranks of the poor and the near poor.

Summary

The wide dispersions of income and wealth in American society, the erosion of the traditional family structure, the essentiality of strong formal education to attain employment at family-sustaining wages, and less than generous social welfare assistance have all combined to maintain poverty at a substantial level, whatever the fluctuations of prosperity. Within that comparatively high level of poverty by the standards of the developed world, few of those born into poverty or condemning themselves to it by personal choices (such as substance abuse, out-of-wedlock birth, or lack of education) escape it by far or for long. Since few of these events seem to be declining to any substantive degree, the poverty level is not likely to decrease substantially in the near future without sustained full-employment conditions in the labor market, real wage growth across the entire distribution, and public policy efforts to supplement the earnings of the working poor.

5. Approaches to and Consequences of Redefining Poverty

As noted in chapter 1, the existing thresholds of income used by the federal government to identify the poverty status of families and individuals have been subject to growing criticism over the past decade.[1] A wide range of alternative measures and concepts of poverty based on absolute and relative income have been proposed as replacements for the existing poverty income thresholds of the federal government. The rationales for these alternative criteria, the absolute and relative size of these proposed alternative poverty income thresholds, and their implications for the size and demographic/socioeconomic composition of the nation's population in poverty are reviewed in this chapter.

The Initial Challenges of Defining and Measuring Poverty

The issue of defining what poverty meant was confronted in 1964. If a war on poverty was to be declared, the enemy had to be identified and means of determining need and measuring progress had to be invented. After President Johnson's declaration of the War on Poverty, federal staff were confronted with the task of defining and measuring the size of the nation's population in poverty. An interim report by the U.S. Council of Economic Advisers in 1964 relied on a simple definition of poverty that classified as poor all families in 1963 with a pretax money income of less than $3,000 and all single individuals with an income under $1,500.[2] The council's definition of poverty was shortly replaced by a new method developed by Mollie Orshansky of the Social Security Administration.[3] Her work on developing poverty income thresholds for families was conducted during 1963–64 and published in the *Social Security Bulletin* in several articles over the 1964–66 period.[4] The Orshansky method for estimating the size of the population in poverty was adopted by the Office of Economic Opportunity in

1965 as a quasi-official measure of the poverty population, and the method was officially adopted by the federal government in the summer of 1969.

Orshansky's original method for constructing poverty income thresholds first involved estimating the amount of income that would be needed by families of varying sizes and age compositions to purchase a standard food budget as defined by the U.S. Department of Agriculture in the early 1960s. She had her choice between a "low-cost" food budget and an "economy plan" and chose the latter intended for "temporary or emergency use when funds are low." Choice of the low-cost plan would have resulted in a poverty line about 30 percent higher than the chosen economy plan for most family sizes. Estimates of the cost of purchasing that minimum food budget were then multiplied by a factor of 3 to reflect the findings of a 1955 national household food consumption survey revealing that the average U.S. household spent one-third of its aftertax income on food consumed both at home and away.[5]

A family of two adults and two children was the standard. The multiplier was set at higher than 3 for smaller families and persons living alone to compensate for their relatively larger per capita fixed expenses. The poverty threshold was weighted by family size, with a larger family having a higher poverty threshold, and by the age of the householder, with an elderly head presumed to have spending requirements about 10 percent less than those under 65 years of age. The poverty income thresholds vary with the age of the family householder, the number of persons in the family, and the number of children under age 18.[6] Single individuals and families headed by an individual age 65 and older are assigned a poverty income threshold that is 8 percent lower than that for younger householders. Persons living in households with others to whom they are not related are treated as a household of one in identifying their poverty status. On that basis, when first developed for 1963, the poverty threshold for a family of four was an annual income of $3,100.[7] As we noted in chapter 1, that figure was about one-half of the median aftertax income for a family of four at the time. The result of that calculation, with some adjustments for family size and age structure, became the original upper boundary of poverty.

The poverty index based on that "economy food plan" was then etched in stone from the 1960s until now. The poverty guidelines advance annually only as a result of changes in the rate of inflation for consumer goods and services as measured by the U.S. Bureau of Labor Statistics's Consumer Price Index for All Urban Consumers, often referred to by its acronym—the CPI-U.[8] Hence, the poverty threshold in use today assumes that a low-income family survives on the same food menu, both in mix and amounts, that it ate in 1955, that the relative costs of specific items within that food basket are unchanged, and that food costs are still the same proportion of a family's living costs in 1999 as in 1964. Of course, none of that is true. Changes in the poverty thresholds over the intervening years are illustrated in table 1.1, but the standards of living represented by those figures have changed radically over time.

Since the poverty income thresholds were officially adopted in 1969, few substantive changes have been made in the underlying concepts. In 1981, a series of rather modest revisions to the existing concepts eliminated the farm/nonfarm distinctions in poverty thresholds, eliminated the differences between the poverty income thresholds for families headed by men and women, and expanded the family size categories to include separate poverty thresholds for families of seven, eight, and nine or more rather than the "seven or more" category used previously.[9]

The Orshansky-based poverty concepts and measures used by the federal government today are frequently referred to as an absolute income measure of poverty rather than a relative income measure, since the poverty thresholds are not adjusted yearly to take into consideration changes in the standard of living of American families.[10] Adjustments are made to reflect changing price levels but not for productivity gains, increased earnings, rising standards of living, or changes in aspirations. Such shifts in societal norms and expectations, driven by real income gains achieved through greater productivity and greater work effort by families, are not captured by a static poverty measure that is adjusted only for changes in the cost of living over time. Orshansky referred to her method as a "relatively absolute" measure of poverty, since it was based in part on the consumption behavior of the average American household, not on that of the poor alone.[11] Since the 1964 poverty line for a family of four was approximately equal to one-half of the post-tax median income of a family of four and was in close accord with findings of an early 1960s Gallup national opinion poll of the minimum amount of income needed to avoid poverty, those 1964 poverty income thresholds were claimed to contain elements of absolute, relative, and subjective poverty definitions.[12]

Static and relative poverty indexes address two distinctly different concerns, and it is actually possible for one index to show an increase in poverty while the other indicates a diminution. A static measure like the official index reveals how the fortunes of low-income households have changed and demonstrates that we made substantial progress during the 1960s and early 1970s in lifting families above a fixed (albeit somewhat arbitrary) minimum income standard. Poverty rates rose during the 1970s and have fluctuated in a narrow but slightly higher range since then, as shown in figure 1.1. A relative poverty measure gauges shifts in income distribution, often offering a reminder that we have made little progress in sharing the benefits of a prosperous economy more equitably. Table 1.2 illustrates that relationship by comparing the static official index to one-half of the median income for selected years. While the official rate fluctuated up and down, based on outmoded food expenditures updated by the CPI-U, the difference between the two measures persistently rose as the incomes of the poor fell further and further below the median.

There has also been continuing debate over the extent to which the previous and recently revised CPI-U understates or overstates changes in inflation and the true cost of living.[13] Even though the poverty thresholds have been adjusted to reflect changes in the level of consumer prices, it is too much to expect that consumption patterns and relative prices would stay constant over such a long period of time. By the late 1980s, the costs of other essentials had risen relative to food costs and the consumption expenditure patterns of families had changed so that food expenditures constituted only one-seventh of the average family's expenditures. Multiplying the cost of that original food basket by 7 rather than 3 would more than double the poverty threshold. Housing costs, which in the mid-1960s were assumed to be about one-quarter of a low-income budget, were at the end of the 1990s closer to one-third and rising for the average family and closer to 50 percent for the majority of low-income households unable to receive rental housing assistance. Shifting to a multiplied housing cost base rather than the food cost base would raise the poverty threshold by about one-half. Simply going into the market to price the same package of goods and services considered to represent poverty in 1964 would currently cost 140 percent of today's poverty threshold.[14]

The poverty income thresholds are also not adjusted for differences in the estimated cost of living across regions, states, or local areas. Thus, the poverty line for a family of four is the same regardless of whether the family lives in New York City, the suburbs of Atlanta, or rural Mississippi. Some poverty researchers, including the National Academy of Science's Panel on Poverty and Family Assistance and the authors of this volume, have argued for an adjustment of poverty income thresholds across states and local areas based on the cost of rental housing.[15] Thus, the poverty index, although supposedly but not actually offering a constant yardstick with which to measure progress, is imprecise at best. By varying only for family size and age composition, the threshold ignores both higher prices in inner cities (where many of the poor are concentrated) and the unpurchased food and other resources available to farmers.

If the consumer price index sometimes overstates inflation, as some have argued, that could understate progress against poverty. The household survey used to ascertain the annual poverty rate tends to undercount family income slightly because of under-reporting of some income sources and therefore also exaggerates the extent of impoverishment. On the other hand, census enumerators have a more difficult time contacting the homeless, poor members of racial and ethnic minorities, immigrants, and other populations whose inclusion would increase the poverty count.

Most of the arguments thus far suggest an actual incidence of poverty substantially higher than the official measure. However, there are also offsetting factors defending a lower rate. The official index ignores all of the noncash goods, services, and other benefits provided by antipoverty programs. By focusing solely on a family's gross money income, the poverty index fails to account for differences in tax burdens and other expenses that affect the amount of disposable income available to meet basic needs. The money income measures are estimated pretax; thus, they exclude the effects of payroll taxes and personal income taxes on the disposable incomes of families. A low-income but earning family might be classified as nonpoor, yet have its take-home pay reduced by taxes to a point below the tax-exempt disposable transfer income received through public assistance or Social Security retirement or disability benefits by a family classified as poor. These potential subtractions from the official poverty measure are discussed later in this chapter.

Alternative Poverty Measures

The weaknesses of the official poverty measure have not gone unnoticed. Alternatives have been proposed based on housing costs, updated food costs, various family budgets, and relative incomes. Most knowledgeable observers recognize the inherent limitations of the official poverty threshold, the consumption power of which has never again been measured but is simply advanced each year by the consumer price index. There is at this point no consensus as to the appropriate measure and little political support for any official change in measurement, but alternatives are explored in this chapter to assure the reader's awareness of relevant antipoverty issues.

An Updated Food Consumption–based Poverty Line

Since 1955, when it was discovered that families containing three or more persons spent approximately one-third of their aftertax money incomes on food, the level and composition of the consumption expenditures of U.S. households have changed markedly. Rising real incomes, increased in-kind transfers (food stamps, rental subsidies), and the altered savings behavior of U.S. households have boosted the real consumption expenditures of the average household and reduced the share of consumption expenditures accounted for by food. Findings of the 1999 Consumer Expenditures Survey revealed that the average consumer unit allocated 13.6 percent of their expenditures on food.[16] For consumer units containing two or more persons, food expenditures accounted for 13.9 percent of total consumption expenditures, and families of four spent 14.3 percent of their budget on food items at or away from home. Using the share of food expenditures for a four-person family in 1999 would have yielded a food expenditure multiplier of approximately 7.00 during that year. This multiplier would have generated a poverty line for a family of four that was 2.33 times as high as the poverty line for four-person families during 1999.

Shelter Poverty: A Poverty Line Based on the Cost of Housing

Housing costs, including utilities and maintenance, have replaced food costs as the largest item in the average family's budget, representing 32 percent of the average consumer unit's expenditures in 1999. To illustrate the impact of that fact, consider that the U.S. Department of Housing and Urban Development uses the 40th percentile of the rental distribution in any community as its estimate of the fair market rent for purposes of the Section 8 rental housing subsidy program. Patricia Ruggles and the authors of this chapter have used the values of these fair market rents for specified two-bedroom units to construct a housing-based poverty budget for a four-person family. During the fall of 1997, the average fair market rent for a two-bedroom apartment in the U.S. was $582 per month. Annualizing this monthly rent and multiplying it by a factor of

3.33 (since rent is one-third the average family's budget) to convert it to a family poverty budget for a four-person family would yield a poverty budget of $23,256. That would exceed the current official poverty line for a four-person family by 42 percent.

The monthly values of these fair market rents varied considerably across local housing markets during 1997, ranging from highs of $1,070 in Stamford, Connecticut and Nassau County, New York to a low of $357 in Gadsden, Alabama. In the fall of 2000, the fair market rents for a two-bedroom apartment in the five most expensive metropolitan areas ranged from $1,144 in Westchester County, New York to a high of $1,459 in the San Francisco PMSA.[17] The fair market rents for the same type of housing unit in the five least expensive metropolitan housing markets ranged from $403 in Saint Joseph, Missouri to $372 in Gadsden, Alabama. The existence of such highly divergent rents for given rental housing units across local areas calls for the use of local cost-of-living adjusted poverty lines in estimating the size of the poverty population of states and local areas. Findings in chapter 3 revealed the effects of such rental cost–adjusted poverty lines on the estimated size of the poor population in states during the late 1990s.

The National Research Council Methodology
for Measuring Poverty

Motivated by swelling criticisms of the federal government's poverty measure, the National Research Council of the National Academy of Sciences assembled in the early 1990s a Panel on Poverty and Family Assistance, consisting of recognized scholars in the field. In its 1995 report to the U.S. Congress, the panel recommended a new set of poverty thresholds based on actual expenditures by low-income households five years earlier. Rather than starting with food costs and applying a large food spending multiplier, the panel chose a "basic needs commodity bundle" of food, clothing, and shelter expanded by a small multiplier to represent additional needs such as household supplies, personal care, and non–work-related transportation. The consumer items included among the additional needs determine the size of the spending multiplier. Rather than relying on a 1955 "economy food plan" priced in 1990s terms for determining the food budget, the panel relied on data from the 1989–91 Consumer Expenditure Surveys, advocating that the survey be conducted every year and an average of the most recent three years be used as the household consumption base, with "poverty" being designated as something less than the median level of consumption for these basic needs items.

The panel then proposed comparing to that consumption-based poverty threshold a family's economic resources, consisting of money income from all sources plus near-money benefits from government transfer programs, such as food stamps and housing subsidies, minus out-of-pocket costs associated with earning income, such as child care, medical care and transportation to work, and payroll and income taxes, in order to determine whether the family is in poverty.

The Panel on Poverty and Family Assistance tested its recommended approach by applying it to 1992 data but was not specific in its policy recommendations. However, a research team from the U.S. Bureau of Labor Statistics and the Census Bureau subsequently applied the technique to 1990–95 data, making some calculations more relevant to our current discussion.[18] The above research group derived what they called a basic consumption bundle consisting of food, clothing, shelter and utilities plus transportation and personal care and a second bundle including the same items as the first bundle but with expenditures for education and reading added. These two bundles resulted in a multiplier of the basic food, clothing and shelter budget of 1.15 and 1.25. Families with different incomes spend differing amounts on these basics. Expenditures of households as measured by the Consumer Expenditure survey were arrayed in ventiles (5 percentage point intervals) and the expenditures at the 30th and 35th percentiles were chosen to represent poverty. Applying that formula, the relationship between the official poverty thresholds and the National Research Council approach would be as shown in table 5.1.

For a married-couple family with two children, the NRC poverty

Table 5.1. Comparisons of the Official and the NRC Poverty Thresholds for Selected Family Types under Bundles 1 and 2, 1995

Family Type	Official Threshold	Bundle 1	Percentage of Difference[a]	Bundle 2	Percentage of Difference[a]
Single householder	$7,763	$6,843	88%	$7,382	95%
Married couple	9,933	11,117	112	11,993	121
Plus one child	12,267	13,715	112	14,769	121
Two children	15,455	16,117	104	17,387	113
Three children	18,187	18,374	101	19,822	109
Four children	20,364	20,517	101	22,134	109
Five children	22,809	22,569	99	24,347	107

[a]Bundle as percentage of the official poverty threshold.

threshold under Bundle 2 would have been 13 percent higher than the official poverty threshold in 1995 while a married-couple family with one child would have been assigned a poverty threshold 21 percent higher than their official poverty threshold during that year. While these relative differences in poverty thresholds for families with children may not seem large, when combined with the changes in the treatment of available family income, they would have raised the poverty rate of all married couples from 6.8 percent to 14.7 percent during 1995, a more than doubling of the official poverty rate for such families.

The U.S Bureau of Labor Statistics's Family Budget Series

From the late 1960s through the early 1980s, the U.S. Bureau of Labor Statistics produced annual estimates of the amount of pretax money income needed by an urban family of four and a retired couple to achieve three different standards of living: a lower living standard, an intermediate living standard, and a higher living standard.[19] These BLS family budget standards included estimates of the costs of food, housing, transportation, clothing, personal care, medical care, other consumption items, and the federal, state, and local tax burden (including income, payroll, and property taxes) for families in each of the survey areas across each of the three family budget standards. Estimates of the amount of pretax income needed by urban families to achieve each of the three budget standards were produced for the nation's urban areas as a whole, for all metropolitan areas combined, and for 25 individual metropolitan areas.

BLS subsequently discontinued the family budget series, though the Department of Labor's Employment and Training Administration continued to use it for determining eligibility for some of its employment and training programs, updating the series annually simply by multiplying the values of the lower living standard income levels for each area by changes in the rate of inflation as measured by area changes in the CPI-U. Hence, after providing relevant data through 1981, this series now shares one of the basic limitations of the current poverty income thresholds, the lack of an updated set of budget components. If it were still being currently measured as it was in its heyday, the family budget series would offer a constantly updated compromise between the absolute and the relative income measures of poverty levels. The contents of the consumption bundle would constantly change in keeping with consumer trends, even though there would be no necessary fixed relationship to median family or household income standards.

We have provided an update of the BLS lower living standard income levels for a national urban family of four through 1999. Findings of our analysis for 1999 are displayed in table 5.2. At the time of the 1981 budget survey, the lower living standard income level for a family of four throughout the entire urban United States was estimated to be $15,323. Over the 1981 to 1999 period, the Bureau of Labor Statistics has estimated that the Consumer Price Index for All Urban Consumers rose by approximately 83 percent. Applying this rate of change in inflation to the 1981 lower living standard income level yields a value for the lower living standard budget in 1999 equal to $28,071. During 1999, the average weighted poverty line for a four-person family in the United States was equal to $17,029. A comparison of the 1999 lower living standard income level with the poverty line for a four-person family yields a relative ratio of approximately 165.0, implying that the lower living standard income budget would have required 65 percent more money income than the poverty line for a four-person family during that year. This multiple of 165 percent of the poverty line will be used as one of our alternative measures of income adequacy standards for the country and used to estimate the number of persons and families who failed to achieve income adequacy in recent years.

The values of the BLS lower living standard income levels (LLSIL) varied across metropolitan areas, metropolitan/nonmetropolitan areas, and geographic regions of the country. In its May 2001 updates, the Employment and Training Administration produced estimates of the LLSIL budgets that ranged from a low of $25,300 in nonmetropolitan areas of the South to highs of $30,360 in metropolitan areas of the Northeast region.[20] Across 23 individual metropolitan areas, the values of the LLSIL budgets ranged from a low of $25,680 in the Houston-Galveston-Brazoria PMSA to highs

Table 5.2. Updating the BLS Lower Living Standard Income Level for an Urban Family of Four to 1999

Variable	Value
Lower living standard income level (LLSIL), 1981	$15,323
Percentage of change in CPI-U index, 1981–99	83.2%
Lower living standard income level, 1999	$28,071
Poverty line for a four-person family, 1999	$17,029
Ratio of LLSIL to poverty	164.8

Sources: U.S. Bureau of Labor Statistics (BLS), 1982; *Monthly Labor Review,* 2000.

of $33,000 in the Boston and Seattle PMSA's and $38,540 in Honolulu. These large geographic variations in the estimated cost of achieving a standard of living provide further justification of the need to adjust future poverty standards for differences in the local cost of living. The continued failure to do so distorts the geographic distribution of scarce federal resources for combatting poverty problems.

The Relative Income Approach to Poverty Measures

Poverty measures can be based on an absolute income, a relative income, or a subjective income approach. The existing poverty literature often makes references to these three alternative approaches to the measurement of poverty in any given country. The official poverty measures of the federal government currently in use in the United States reflect the absolute income approach to poverty, i.e., the existing poverty income thresholds for families are based on an absolute amount of money income that is believed to be needed by a family of a given size and age composition to achieve a minimally adequate level of consumption of goods and services. As noted earlier, however, other than general food expenditures, the specific goods and services comprising this poverty budget are not identified. In contrast to this absolute approach, the relative income approach is based on the general notion that the amount of expenditures or income needed by a family to avoid deprivation should be related to the average amount of consumption or income obtained by other families in their local communities or the nation at large. This relative income approach, thus, is based on a relative definition of deprivation.

A rationale for adopting a relative income definition of poverty was made by Adam Smith more than two hundred years ago in his classic economic tome, *The Wealth of Nations*. In discussing the relationships between wages and the prices of necessities, Smith argued that "by necessaries I understand not only the commodities which are indispensably necessary for the support of life, but whatever the custom of the country renders it indecent for creditable people, even of the lowest order, to be without . . . a creditable day-laborer would be ashamed to appear in public without a linen shirt, the want of which would be supposed to denote that disgraceful degree of poverty."[21]

In more modern times, the case for adopting a relative income approach has been made by poverty researchers in the United Kingdom, other Western European nations, and the United States. In an early 1960s article on "The Meaning of Poverty," Peter

Townsend, a British sociologist, made the following case for a relative income approach to poverty measurement: "Poverty is a dynamic not a static concept. Man is not a Robinson Crusoe living on a desert island . . . Our general theory, then, should be that individuals and families whose resources over time fall seriously short of the resources commanded by the average individual or family in the community in which they live, whether that community is a local, national, or international one, are in poverty."[22]

In the late 1960s, Victor Fuchs, a U.S. economist, also argued in favor of the use of a relative income approach to poverty, claiming that adoption of the relative approach would allow the nation to simultaneously address income distribution problems. Fuchs also provided a very specific definition of relative poverty. "I propose that we define as poor any family whose income is less than one-half the median family income. No special claim is made for the precise figure of one-half; but the advantages of using a poverty standard that changes with the growth of real national income are considerable."[23]

In his recent review of *The Real Worlds of Welfare Capitalism,* Robert Solow, an MIT economist and Nobel Prize laureate, made the following observations on the adequacy of the current poverty income thresholds in the United States: "Median family income in the U.S. is currently about $45,000 (in 1998). By the relative standard, families would qualify *as very poor* if their incomes were lower than $18,000, so our poverty line actually represents a lower standard of living than what a European would call deep poverty in the relative sense."[24]

Comparisons of the values of the existing poverty income thresholds for families of varying sizes with those that would prevail under a relative income approach to poverty measurement would be illuminating. In its 1995 report to the U.S. Congress, the National Research Council's Panel on Poverty and Family Assistance compared the value of the 1963 poverty line for a four-person family in the United States with the median pretax and post-tax money incomes of such families. They found that the 1963 official poverty line for a family of four was equivalent to 43.5 percent of the pretax money income and 50 percent of the post-tax median income for a four-person family.[25]

We have utilized March Current Population Survey (CPS) data on the estimated median incomes of four-person families in the United States for selected years from 1964 to 1999 to compare the changing relative values of the federal government's poverty income thresholds for four person families. The poverty thresholds are only updated annually to reflect estimated changes in the cost of living as represented by the CPI-U. In 1964, the average weighted poverty line for a four-person family was equal to 42.3 percent of the pretax median money income of such families (table 5.3). This ratio fell to 35 percent by the end of the 1960s and to just under 33 percent at the end of the 1970s as a consequence of rising real incomes of families. During the 1980s, this ratio declined only modestly to 31 percent due to modest growth in the median real incomes of families during that decade. By 1999, the ratio had declined to a new low of 28.4 percent.

To restore the 1999 poverty line for a family of four to its 1963 relationship to the median pretax income for families of such size, we would have to raise it to $26,091, which is equal to 153 percent of its 1999 level. Similar calculations based on the post-tax, median incomes of families of four revealed that the 1999 official poverty line for four person families was equal to only 33 percent of the $51,380 median value of post-tax money income for such families. To restore the 1999 poverty line for four person families to its comparative relationship with the post-tax median money income of such families in 1963, we would have to raise it by 51 percent to $25,690.

In table 5.4, we present comparisons of the 1999 poverty income thresholds for families containing two to seven persons with the median, pretax money incomes of such families. During 1999, the poverty lines for families containing two to three persons were equivalent to only 26 percent of their median family incomes, however, the poverty line's percentage share of median family incomes rose to nearly 37 percent for families containing 5 persons and to nearly 50 percent for families with 7 persons.[26]

If a relative definition of poverty were adopted similar to that proposed by Victor Fuchs and applied separately to families of

Table 5.3. Median Pretax Money Incomes and Weighted Average Poverty Thresholds of U.S. Four-Person Families, 1964–1999 (in Current Dollars)

Year	Poverty Line	Median Income	Poverty/ Income
1964	$3,169	$7,488	42.3%
1969	3,743	10,623	35.2
1979	7,412	22,512	32.9
1989	12,674	40,763	31.1
1992	14,335	44,251	32.4
1999	17,029	59,981	28.4

Table 5.4. Comparisons of the Median Pretax Money Incomes and Weighted Average Poverty Thresholds of U.S. Families by Family Size, 1999

No. in Family	Median Income	Weighted Average Poverty Threshold	Poverty Threshold as Percentage of Median Income
2	$41,512	$10,869	26.2%
3	50,400	13,290	26.4
4	60,000	17,029	28.4
5	54,878	20,127	36.6
6	51,086	22,727	44.5
7	52,000	25,912	49.8

Sources: U.S. Census Bureau, March 2000 Current Population Survey public use files, tabulations by authors; U.S. Census Bureau, Current Population Reports, Series P60-290, *Poverty in the United States, 1999.*

Table 5.5. Calculating a New Set of Poverty Income Thresholds for Families Based on a Relative Income Definition by Family Size, 1999

Family Size	New Poverty Line[a]	Old Poverty Line	New as Percentage of Old
2	$20,756	$10,869	191%
3	25,200	13,290	190
4	30,000	17,029	176
5	27,439	20,127	136
6	25,543	22,727	112
7	26,000	25,912	100

[a]New poverty line is equal to 50% of the pretax median money income of all families in the given family size category.

each size from 2 to 7 persons, the new poverty lines for such families would range from $20,756 for families of two to a high of $30,000 for a family of four (table 5.5). Given the lower median incomes of larger families in the United States in 1999, one ends up with the anomalous finding that their relative poverty income thresholds would actually be lower than those of families of four. These relative poverty income thresholds based on 50 percent of the median pretax money incomes of families in each family size category would range from 100 percent of the existing poverty income thresholds for families containing seven persons to 190 percent for families containing only two or three persons. If the findings for families in each size category are weighted by their share of all families in the United States in 1999, the weighted average relative poverty line for families would be equal to 178 percent of the current federal poverty income thresholds.

The Public's Subjective Perceptions of Appropriate Poverty and Minimum Income Adequacy Standards

A third approach to the formulation of poverty income guidelines or thresholds involves the use of public opinion polls to ascertain the general public's views on appropriate poverty income criteria.[27] Over the past two decades, national and local public opinion surveys have attempted to identify the public's views with respect to the amounts of income needed by a family to avoid poverty or to achieve a desired minimum standard of living. Findings of these surveys have consistently revealed that the American public has a subjective average poverty standard that is typically from 130 percent to 200 percent of the federal government's poverty income thresholds for various family sizes. Use of these more subjective poverty income thresholds would yield higher estimates of the numbers of poor persons and families in the United States, though no serious proposal has suggested using these surveys as a basis for legislative or administrative determination of the appropriate poverty threshold.[28]

Offsetting Factors

Most of the arguments thus far have suggested an actual incidence of poverty substantially higher than the official measure. However, there are also offsetting factors defending a lower rate. The official index ignores all of the noncash goods, services, and other benefits that the poor may receive. As the poverty income threshold was promulgated in 1964, cash public assistance from the Aid to Families with Dependent Children (AFDC) program existed, but many of the programs aiding low-income families that were to be the products of the coming "war on poverty" did not. Although the sum of food stamps, health care, subsidized housing, and other needs-tested assistance that did not then exist now accounts for more than three-fourths of all federal aid to the poor, the value of this in-kind aid is ignored in the official poverty count. Table 5.6 illustrates this fact with data for various years from 1979–98, taking into account the cash value of employer-provided benefits, non–means-tested noncash benefits including food stamps, housing, school lunch, and the fungible value of Medicaid and adding

Table 5.6. Effects of Federal Noncash Benefits and Taxes on the Poverty Rate

Year	Official Poverty Rate	Poverty Rate with Noncash Benefits	Percentage Reduction
1979	11.7%	7.9%	32.5%
1983	15.2	11.0	27.6
1989	12.8	8.9	30.5
1990	13.5	9.5	29.6
1991	14.2	9.9	30.3
1992	14.8	10.5	29.1
1993	15.1	10.7	29.1
1994	14.5	9.8	29.7
1995	13.8	9.0	34.8
1996	13.7	8.9	35.0
1997	13.3	8.8	33.8
1998	12.7	8.2	35.4

Source: House Committee on Ways and Means, *2000 Green Book: Background Material and Data on Programs within the Jurisdiction of the Committee on Ways and Means* (Washington, D.C.: U.S. Government Printing Office, 2000), 1291.

in the effects of state and federal taxes. Those who receive health insurance from their employer and those eligible for Medicaid or Medicare have more to spend on other needs than those who have to buy medical care. The same can be said for the costs of transportation to work, of clothing to attend work or for child care to be able to work. The money income measure also excludes capital gains—not important to most of the poor—and payments under the federal and state Earned Income Tax Credit (EITC)—increasingly important to them.[29]

In summary, the most serious limitation of the current official poverty index is its lack of any stable relationship over time to some accepted living standard for the nation's families. Though apparently not chosen deliberately for that reason, when it was introduced nearly four decades ago, the poverty index based on the food cost criteria of Mollie Orshansky was about equal to one-half of the national median post-tax family income for a four-person family. In 1999, the poverty line for a four-person family was equal to only one-third of the median post-tax income for four person families. For families of two to three persons, the poverty lines represented even lower shares of their post-tax incomes. To restore the poverty line for a four-person family to the relative position of 1963, it would have to be raised by 50 percent. To repeat what we

Table 5.7. Percentage of Persons with Incomes below 50 Percent of the Median Family Income Compared to Percentage of Persons with Incomes below the Official Poverty Rate, 1969–1998

Year	Persons with Income 50% of Median	Official Poverty Rate	Difference between Official Poverty Rate and 50% Median
1969	17.9%	12.1%	5.8%
1979	20.0	11.7	8.3
1989	22.0	12.8	9.2
1998	22.3	12.7	9.6

Source: Mishel, Bernstein, and Schmitt, *The State of Working America, 2000–2001,* p. 299.

said in the first chapter, if the poverty level were returned to the 50 percent of median post-tax family income where it was in 1964, 56.8 million people would have been considered poor in 1999 rather than the 32.3 million measured as poor in that year by the current criterion. In 1998, rather than 12.7 percent, the poverty rate would have been 22.3 percent, almost equal to its 1959 level (table 5.7). Only a poverty threshold retaining one-half of the post-tax median income as it did in 1964 could have allowed the poor to share at least conceptually in society's economic progress over that long period of time.

All of these factors are important both in deciding who is and who is not poor and how many are poor. To address these shortcomings in the existing poverty concepts and measures, the U.S. Census Bureau has produced an array of alternative poverty rates based on adjustments to the existing measures that take into account capital gains, imputed rental income on owned homes, in-kind benefits, EITC payments, and payroll and personal income taxes.[30] However, since it is difficult to place a monetary value on these noncash benefits and since the various individuals and families receive widely varying quantities of each with varying effects upon their standards of living, there is no simple way of including them in any single poverty index.

The Range of Alternative Poverty Income Measures

The preceding discussions of alternative replacements for the existing poverty income thresholds of the federal government have revealed a rather diverse array of income measures and values. In table 5.8, we display eight of the alternative replacement measures and the degree to which each of these poverty income measures would exceed the value of the current poverty income thresholds for various family types, primarily families containing four persons. The values of these eight alternative poverty measures range from 113 percent of the existing poverty lines to 233 percent of the current poverty income thresholds of the federal government.

Everyone who has seriously examined the issue appears to agree that the official federal policy threshold should be increased. The remaining issues are only how much to increase the threshold and, politically, how to get it done.

Table 5.8. Justifications for Selected Alternative Measures of Family Poverty Income Thresholds in the United States

Poverty Line Multiple	Studies Presenting This Justification
1.13	National Research Council's Panel on Poverty and Family Assistance method based on actual consumption expenditures by low-income families in 1990–95 (family of 4)
1.28–1.30	1989 Gallup Poll findings of income needed by a family of 4 to avoid poverty in the U.S. Northeast region
1.50	50% of the post-tax median income for families of 4 in 1999 or 43% of the pretax median income for families of 4 in 1999
1.65	Ratio of the CPI-U-adjusted Bureau of Labor Statistics lower living standard income level for a family of 4 to the average weighted poverty threshold for such families in 1999
1.76	Median response to a 1992 Gallup survey of minimum income to get along as a percentage of the 4-person poverty line
1.78	Weighted ratio of one-half of the median pretax incomes of 2–7-person families to their poverty thresholds
2.10	1990 and 1994 median responses to national Roper Poll questions on the minimum income needed by a family to "just get by" as a percentage of the 3-person poverty line
2.33	Food spending multiplier raised to 7 as represented by the share of consumption expenditures spent on food by the average U.S. 4-person family in 1999

The Effects of Alternative Poverty Measures on the Estimated Number of Poor Families and Persons

Each proposed alternative replacement for the existing poverty income thresholds of the federal government has consequences for the estimated size and demographic/socioeconomic characteristics of the nation's and regions' "poverty" populations. To illustrate how the magnitude of the poverty population varies by definition of poverty, we have generated estimates of the percentage of U.S. families and persons that would have been classified as poor under three alternative multiples of the poverty line: 100 percent, 150 percent, and 165 percent. For 1999, we also provide estimates of the number of poor families at 133 percent and 200 percent of the poverty line.

Trends in the percentage of U.S. families with pretax money incomes at 100 percent, 150 percent, and 165 percent of the poverty line during the 1990s are portrayed in table 5.9. Family poverty rates rose in the early 1990s as a consequence of the recession of 1989–90 and the jobless recovery of 1990–91. After peaking in 1993 at 12.3 percent, the family poverty rate fell steadily over the remainder of the decade, declining to 9.3 percent by 1999 and 8.6 percent in 2000. In 1991, nearly one of every five families had a money income below 150 percent of the poverty line. The strength of the U.S. economy generated rising real family incomes after 1993 helped lower the share of families with incomes below 150 percent, but it was not as effective in lowering the share of such families as it was in reducing the official count of poor families (−11% vs. −19% to 1999). In 1991, 22 percent of all U.S. families had an income below 165 percent of the poverty line, nearly dou-

Table 5.9. Trends in the Percentage of U.S. Families with Annual Pretax Money Incomes below Specified Multiples of the Poverty Line, Selected Years, 1991–1999

Poverty Line Multiple	1991	1995	1996	1997	1999	Percentage Point Change, 1991–99
1.00	11.5%	10.8%	11.0%	10.3%	9.3%	−2.2%
1.50	19.4	19.0	19.1	18.1	17.2	−2.2
1.65	22.0	21.8	21.9	20.9	19.6	−2.4

Source: March Current Population Survey public use tapes, 1992, 1996, 1997, 1998, and 2000 tabulations by the Center for Labor Market Studies, Northeastern University.

ble the incidence of official poverty problems. By the end of the decade, the share of families with income below 165 percent of the poverty line had fallen to 19.6 percent, but this represented only a 2.4 percentage point reduction. Again, in relative terms, this represented a reduction only about one-half as high as that for the official poverty rate. The rising economic tide of the 1990s was more effective in lowering the official poverty rate than in reducing the number of families with incomes below 165 percent of the poverty line, the equivalent of the BLS lower living standard income level for a four-person urban family.

How many families in the United States would have fallen below our alternative poverty definitions in 1999? During that year, nearly 6.7 million families had money incomes below 100 percent of the poverty line (table 5.10). The number of families with incomes below 133 percent of the poverty line was 10.3 million, would have risen to nearly 14.1 million if the 165 percent multiple had been used, and would have increased to 18.6 million families if 200 percent of the poverty line were used as the appropriate criteria.[31] The number of families with incomes below 165 percent of the poverty line was 2.11 times as high as the number of officially poor families, and the number of families with an income below 200 percent of the poverty line was 2.8 times as high

Table 5.10. Estimated Number of U.S. Families with Incomes below Specified Multiples of the Poverty Line under Three Alternative Income Measures, 1999

	No. of Families (in 1000s)		
Poverty Multiplier	*Money Income Pretax*	*Money Income plus EITC and In-kind Benefits*	*Money Income plus EITC and In-kind Benefits Less Personal Taxes*
1.00	6,674	4,912	5,256
1.33	10,307	7,923	8,614
1.50	12,359	9,759	10,840
1.65	14,088	11,596	12,885
2.00	18,605	16,076	18,261
Ratio of 1.65 to 1.00 × Poverty Line	2.11	2.36	2.45
Ratio of 2.00 to 1.00 × Poverty Line	2.79	3.27	3.47

Abbreviation: EITC, Earned Income Tax Credit.

**Table 5.11. Percentage of Families in U.S. Geographic Divisions with Money
Incomes below Specified Multiples of the Official Poverty Threshold, 1999**

Geographic Division	(A) 1.00 × Poverty	(B) 1.33 × Poverty	(C) 1.50 × Poverty	(D) 1.65 × Poverty	Ratio of Col. D/Col. A
New England	7.2%	11.4%	13.8%	16.0%	2.23
Middle Atlantic	9.4	14.4	16.9	19.2	2.05
East North Central	7.6	11.4	14.0	15.8	2.08
West North Central	7.8	12.2	14.3	16.1	2.07
South Atlantic	8.7	13.6	16.5	19.5	2.24
East South Central	11.4	17.5	21.0	23.7	2.39
West South Central	12.5	17.8	21.4	24.4	1.95
Mountain	8.6	14.0	17.3	19.7	2.28
Pacific	10.1	16.3	19.3	21.4	2.12

Source: March 2000 Current Population Survey public use files, tabulations by Center for Labor Market Studies.

as the number of families with money incomes below the official poverty line. Clearly, the choice of an appropriate poverty income threshold has critical implications for the estimated size of the nation's poverty population and for determining progress in combatting poverty problems over time.

To identify how the use of alternative poverty income criteria will influence the estimated size of the poverty population in different geographic areas of the nation, we estimated the share of families with money incomes below 100 percent, 133 percent, 150 percent, and 165 percent of the poverty line in each of the nine geographic divisions of the nation during 1999 (table 5.11). In each of the nine geographic divisions, the more realistic higher indices typically exceeded the official poverty rate by 2 or more times. While the official family poverty rates in these nine geographic divisions ranged from 7 to 12 percent during 1999, the share of families with incomes below 165 percent of the poverty line ranged from a low of 16 percent in New England to highs of 24 percent in the East South Central and West South Central regions. Clearly, any effort to move to a new, higher set of poverty income guidelines will substantially affect the size of the poverty population in every major geographic region of the country. Yet each of these higher levels is a more accurate rendering of the poverty concept introduced in 1964 than the measure currently in use.

Poverty Line Revisions and Their Consequences for the Number of Poor Persons

Any revisions in the income criteria used to define poverty in the United States will have even more dramatic consequences for the estimates of the number of poor persons in the nation than of estimates of the numbers of families. Since unrelated individuals have higher poverty rates than persons living in family households and since the poverty rates of families tend to rise with family size, the poverty rate of all persons regardless of income criteria exceeds that of families. As revealed earlier in chapter 2, the official poverty rate of all persons rose during the early 1990s peaking at 15.1 percent in 1993. By 1999, the official poverty rate had declined to 11.8 percent, a reduction of 16 percent from its 1991 rate (table 5.12). (The official poverty rate had declined to 11.3% by 2000.) The fraction of the population with incomes below 150 percent and 165 percent of the poverty line varied within a much more narrow range over this time period. The share of the population with money incomes below 150 percent of the poverty line fell by only 7 percent between 1991 and 1999 while the share of the population with incomes below 165 percent of the poverty line declined by only 6 percent over the same time period. During 1999, while only 12 percent of the population had incomes below the official poverty line, nearly one-fourth of the nation's residents lived in households with incomes below 165 percent of the poverty line.

Estimates of the total number of persons with incomes below selected multiples of the poverty line during 1999 are displayed in table 5.13. Based simply on their pretax, money incomes, 32.6 million residents of the United States were classified as poor. If the

Table 5.12. Trends in the Percentage of Persons with Annual Incomes below Specified Multiples of the Poverty Line, Selected Years, 1991–1999

Poverty Line Multiple	Persons with Incomes below Poverty Line				Percentage of Change, 1991–99
	1991	1995	1997	1999	
1.00	14.3%	14.0%	13.4%	12.0%	−16%
1.50	23.8	23.7	22.6	22.2	−7%
1.65	26.6	26.8	25.6	24.8	−6%

Source: March 1992, 1996, 1998, and 2000 Current Population Survey, tabulations by Center for Labor Market Studies.

Table 5.13. Estimated Number of Persons in the United States with Incomes below Specified Multiples of the Poverty Line under Three Alternative Income Measures

	Persons with Incomes below Poverty Line (in 1000s)		
Poverty Multiple	*Money Income Pretax*	*Money Income plus EITC and In-kind Benefits*	*Money Income plus EITC and In-kind Benefits less Personal Taxes*
1.00	32,616	29,957	31,081
1.33	51,528	43,799	46,184
1.50	60,847	52,378	55,667
1.65	67,973	59,806	63,670
Ratio of 1.65 to 1.00 × Poverty Line	2.08	2.00	2.05

Source: March 2000 Current Population Survey public use data files, tabulations by Center for Labor Market Studies.
Abbreviation: EITC, Earned Income Tax Credit.

poverty income criterion is raised to 133 percent of the poverty line (approximately the same as the general public's view of the poverty line in the late 1980s), then the number of poor persons would rise to 51.5 million. The use of a 150 percent poverty income standard (the poverty income cutoff for a four-person family using a relative definition of poverty pegged to 50 percent of the median post-tax income of a family of four) would raise the size of the poor population to just under 61 million, and the use of the 165 percent multiple would increase the size of the poor population to nearly 68 million. Thus, use of the 165 percent poverty line multiple to identify the poor would have more than doubled the size of the poverty population in 1999.

The Effects of Alternative Poverty Income Criteria on the Demographic and Socioeconomic Composition of the Poor

Revising the income criteria used to define poverty also will have consequences for the demographic and socioeconomic characteristics of the poor.[32] To illustrate the potential effects of revising the poverty income criteria to 165 percent of the current poverty line, we estimated the fraction of U.S. families in various demographic/ socioeconomic subgroups who had money incomes below 165 percent of the poverty line in selected years during the 1990s and

compared the percentage distribution of families with incomes below the official poverty line with that for families with incomes below 165 percent of the poverty line during 1999. The latter set of
findings will enable us to identify how our perception of "who"
the poor are changes with the definition of poverty.

During each year in the 1990s, the share of families with incomes below 165 percent of the poverty line varied quite considerably by the age of the family householder (table 5.14). Families
headed by an individual under the age of 25 were the most likely
by far to have an income under 165 percent of the poverty line,
with a slight majority of all such families being poor in each year,
except 1999 during which the percentage of young families with
an income below 165 percent of the poverty line fell modestly below 50 percent. The incidence of such poverty problems declines
with the age of the family householder until the age group 55–64

**Table 5.14. Percentage of U.S. Families with Incomes below 165%
of the Poverty Line by Selected Demographic and Socioeconomic
Characteristics of the Family Householder, Selected Years, 1991–1999**

Characteristic of Householder	*1991*	*1995*	*1996*	*1997*	*1999*
All	22.0%	21.8%	21.9%	20.9%	19.6%
Age group					
<25	52.9	54.0	52.9	50.6	48.9
25–34	30.7	30.2	31.0	29.3	27.7
35–44	19.7	21.1	21.1	20.7	19.1
45–54	13.7	13.4	13.4	12.7	12.2
55–64	16.1	16.4	161.1	14.4	14.9
65+	21.0	18.8	19.8	19.3	16.5
Race/ethnic group					
Black, non-Hispanic	46.2	42.8	43.2	40.9	38.1
Hispanic	45.7	48.7	46.8	44.9	41.2
Asian/Pacific Islander	26.6	27.1	25.1	20.4	20.3
White, non-Hispanic	15.9	15.2	15.3	14.7	13.8
Educational attainment					
<12 yr	45.7	47.5	47.2	46.8	45.2
12 yr	23.1	23.2	23.7	22.6	22.1
13–15 yr	15.3	17.2	17.2	16.4	15.5
16+ yr	5.2	5.8	6.1	5.3	4.9
Weeks of work in prior year					
Did not work last year	39.7	37.7	38.5	35.7	31.8
Worked less than 27 wk	46.1	44.8	45.6	45.3	43.6
Worked 40 or more wk	12.6	13.4	13.2	12.8	12.9

is reached, when the incidence begins to rise. The nation's elderly families were the most substantially affected by a shift to a higher poverty income standard. In 1999, they represented only 9 percent of all poor families, but they accounted for nearly 14 percent of all families with an income below 165 percent of the existing poverty income thresholds.

The likelihood of a family having an income below 165 percent of the poverty line varied considerably by the race-ethnic group of the family householder each year during the 1990s. Black and Hispanic families were nearly 3 times as likely as white non-Hispanic families to fall below this income adequacy standard each year (table 5.15). However, as the poverty income criterion is raised from 100 percent to 165 percent of the official poverty line, white, non-Hispanic families are more substantially affected. For exam-

Table 5.15. Percentage Distribution of U.S. Families with Incomes below the Poverty Line and 165% of the Poverty Line by Selected Demographic Characteristics of the Family Householder, 1999

Characteristic of Householder	(A) Income below Poverty Line	(B) Income under 165%	Ratio of Col. B/Col. A
All	100.0%	100.0%	100.0%
Age group			
<25	14.7	11.6	79
25–34	27.8	25.6	92
35–44	24.5	25.3	103
45–54	13.4	13.7	102
55–64	10.5	10.1	96
65+	9.0	13.6	150
Race			
White, not Hispanic	44.4	49.6	112
Black, not Hispanic	27.2	22.3	82
Hispanic	22.8	21.8	96
Asian	3.7	3.5	95
Educational attainment			
≤12, no diploma	40.1	36.3	90
12, diploma or equivalent	35.3	36.0	102
13–15	18.4	21.1	115
16	4.4	4.8	111
16+	1.7	1.7	101
Weeks of work in prior year			
Did not work last year	45.7	40.1	88
Worked less than 27 wk	17.8	12.1	68
Worked more than 40 wk			

ple, during calendar year 1999, only 44 percent of the nation's poor families were headed by a white, non-Hispanic; however, they represented 50 percent of all of the nation's families with an income below 165 percent of the poverty line.

The incidence of family income inadequacy problems throughout the 1990s was strongly associated with the educational attainment of the family householder. Forty-five percent or more of all families with a householder lacking a high school diploma or a GED certificate had an income below 165 percent of the poverty line each year during the 1990s, and there was no significant decline in the fraction of such families with an income inadequacy problem between 1991 and 1999. Approximately 2 of every 9 families with a householder possessing a high school diploma (or GED certificate) but no postsecondary schooling failed to obtain an income above 165 percent of the poverty line during the 1990s as did one of every six families with a householder completing 13 to 15 years of school. In contrast, only 5 percent of the nation's families headed by an individual with a bachelor's or more advanced degree failed to obtain an income above 165 percent of the poverty line. It should be noted that there were no statistically significant declines in the incidence of income inadequacy problems among families within each of our four educational groups during the 1990s. The small decline in the overall incidence of such problems between 1991 and 1999 was entirely attributable to improvements in the educational attainment of the nation's family householders over the decade.

The likelihood of a family having an income below 165 percent of the poverty line also was strongly associated with the intensity of the work effort of the family householder. During the 1990s, typically 35 to 40 percent of the nation's families with a nonworking householder had an income below 165 percent of the poverty line.[33] Among those families with an employed householder who worked six months or less, 44 to 46 percent of them experienced an income inadequacy problem during the 1990s. In contrast, only 12 to 13 percent of those families with a householder who worked 40 or more weeks failed to obtain an income above 165 percent of the poverty line. The latter members of the "working poor," however, comprised a much larger fraction of the families with incomes below 165 percent of the poverty line than they did of the official poor. During 1999, only 30 percent of the nation's officially poor families were headed by an individual who worked 40 or more weeks during the year; however, these same working poor families accounted for 43 percent of the nation's families with incomes below 165 percent of the poverty line. Broadening the definition of poverty would disproportionately increase the numbers of the "working poor" and provide greater incentives for policymakers at the national, state, and local levels to extend more financial assistance to them than is currently provided today, including expanded health insurance coverage, rental subsidy assistance, and more liberal Earned Income Tax Credits.

The Relationship of In-Kind Benefits, EITC Tax Credits, and Payroll and Income Taxes to Poverty Multiples

The money income measure of the U.S. Census Bureau includes a wide array of cash income sources, but excludes federal and state Earned Income Tax Credits, which are the equivalent of cash income, and many "near cash in-kind" transfers, such as food stamps, rental housing subsidies, subsidized or free lunches for school children, and Medicare/Medicaid benefits. The money income measures of the U.S. Census Bureau also are measured pretax while the expenditures needed to finance the consumption bundles underlying many of the poverty income measures must be financed out of disposable income. Exclusion of the EITC payments and in-kind benefits from the money income of the family will exaggerate the true extent of poverty in the nation while the failure to adjust the money income measures for payroll and federal and state income taxes will underestimate poverty problems for some groups, especially when the higher poverty multipliers are used to define poverty. Potential cash payments to low-income working families under the federal EITC program were substantially expanded by the U.S. Congress in 1993. As of 2000, an eligible family with one child could receive a maximum of $2,353 in EITC payments while an eligible family with two children could receive up to $3,888 in rebates from the federal government.[34]

In recent years, the U.S. Census Bureau has made efforts to incorporate Earned Income Tax Credits, the value of in-kind benefits, and selected taxes into alternative poverty income measures.[35] In addition, the U.S. Census Bureau has provided estimates of the values of these in-kind benefits, Earned Income Tax Credits, and payroll and income taxes on the March CPS public use data files. We have used the values for some of these in-kind benefits and taxes to re-estimate the number and percentage of families with adjusted incomes below various multiples of the poverty line. Our two adjusted income measures take into account the following variables:

1. Money income plus in-kind benefits and EITC payments, including food stamps, rental housing subsidies, and the fungible value of Medicare and Medicaid benefits.

2. Money income plus EITC credits and in-kind benefits less payroll taxes paid by the worker, federal government retirement contributions, state income taxes, and federal income taxes.

Estimates of the percentage of U.S. families with adjusted money incomes at or below selected multiples of the poverty line in 1999 are displayed in table 5.16. When EITC payments and in-kind benefits are included in the money income measures of families, the family poverty rates in 1999 ranged from 6.8 percent for 100 percent of the poverty line to 13.6 percent for 150 percent of the poverty line to 22.1 percent for 200 percent of the poverty line. The poverty-reducing effect of the inclusion of EITC credits and in-kind benefits in family income is greatest for those families with money incomes below the poverty line. The family poverty rate is reduced by 2.5 percentage points, or 27 percent, when such benefits are included as income; however, when the poverty income thresholds are raised to 200 percent of the poverty line, the inclusion of such benefits only lowers the poverty rate by one additional percentage point, due to the fact that relatively few working poor families with money incomes above 133 percent of the current poverty lines receive any of these benefits.

Adjusting the money incomes of families to exclude payroll taxes, federal pension contributions, and state and federal income taxes raises the estimated incidence of poverty problems at each alternative poverty income threshold, with the largest effects felt at the higher income thresholds. The incidence of family poverty problems for our most comprehensive income measure ranges from 7.3 percent for the 100 percent poverty standard to 15 percent for the 150 percent of poverty standard, to 25 percent for our 200 percent of poverty standard (table 5.16). One of every four U.S. families failed to achieve an adjusted, post-tax income above 200 percent of the poverty line in 1999. There were 18,261,000 such families in the nation during that year. Their numbers did not shrink during the economic boom years of the mid- to late 1990s. The strong economy together with expanded EITC tax credits was more successful in raising families out of official poverty than in bringing them above the 200 percent of poverty threshold, adjusted for both in-kind benefits and payroll and income taxes.

Table 5.16. Percentage of U.S. Families with Incomes below Specific Multiples of the Official Poverty Threshold, Excluding and Including In-kind Benefits and Personal Taxes, 1999

	Families with Incomes below Poverty Line		
Poverty Multiple	*Money Income Pretax*	*Money Income plus EITC and In-kind Benefits*	*Money Income plus EITC and In-kind Benefits less Personal Taxes*
1.00	9.3%	6.8%	7.3%
1.33	14.3	11.0	12.0
1.50	17.2	13.6	15.0
1.65	19.6	16.1	17.9
2.00	25.6	22.1	25.2
Percentage of Change from 1.00 to 2.00 × Poverty Threshold	+175%	+225%	+245%

Source: March 2000 Current Population Survey public use data files, tabulations by Center for Labor Market Studies.

Note: Number of families as of March 2000. EITC, Earned Income Tax Credit.

Linkages to Labor Market Data

Our understanding of the level and causes of poverty also can be enhanced through the use of measures that link poverty and employment data and provide a more comprehensive picture of labor market conditions and problems. The official poverty index alone fails to reveal whether the poor suffer deprivation as a result of low wages, lack of job opportunities, or nonparticipation in the labor force. A labor market-related economic hardship measure could shed light on these important questions, yielding valuable information on levels of employment and earnings among the poor as well as on the extent of deprivation among the unemployed and underemployed.

Reporting on Labor Day, 1979, the National Commission on Employment and Unemployment Statistics, chaired by the late Sar Levitan, recommended the launching of such a "hardship index." In response to what became known thereafter as the Levitan Report, the U.S. Bureau of Labor Statistics (BLS) published annual reports on "employment problems and economic status" for the years 1979–82, dropping the series thereafter, claiming that public and professional interest in the data were lacking. In 1983, the

Census Bureau inaugurated a Survey of Income and Program Participation (SIPP), which provides some data linking economic hardship with labor force status. Then in 1989 the BLS resumed publishing an annual Profile of the Working Poor, the first covering data from 1987 and the most recent report covering data to 1999.[36] The focus of these reports has been on workers who spent more than half the year in the labor force, either working or looking for work, but remained in poverty. In 1999 such workers numbered 6.8 million, or 32 percent of all persons 16 and older in the Census Bureau poverty count.

Such findings make clear that the incidence of poverty in the United States extends well beyond the indigent into working families. Robert Haveman and Lawrence Buron have calculated that, even if the adult members of every American family were making the fullest use of their physical and human capital in the labor market, nearly 7 percent of the population would still be poor. In other words, the state of the labor market, together with the earning capacity of the population, has created a situation in which more than one out of fifteen Americans must be poor, no matter how hard they work.[37] That may help explain in part why, despite all of the changes that have occurred in the U.S. economy over the past 40 years, poverty has indeed been the persistent lot of between one out of seven and one out of nine Americans. But we are once again reminded that, had the poverty measure retained its 1964 relationship to median family income, the proportion in 2000 would have been more like one out of five.

Summary

As we said in the first chapter, we have, to a substantial extent, lowered poverty rates in the United States over the past 38 years by either redefining the terms or eliminating any contextual definition. In pursuit of the War on Poverty, we have indeed, to a degree, "declared victory and gone home." Antipoverty policies would be more meaningful if either the relative income basis of the original criteria were reintroduced or a new definition, which provided a more realistic estimate of the income needed to achieve a minimum standard of living, was endorsed. But existing antipoverty policies are based on the existing poverty thresholds. This chapter reminds the reader that surmounting the current poverty line is a long way from attaining a family-sustaining income, which, after all, should be the goal of antipoverty policy.

6. Is Poverty in the United States Inescapable?

After declining by one-half between 1959 and 1973, the official poverty rates for persons and families in the United States have shown no further long-term decline, being subject only to cyclical swings. Despite nine consecutive years of strong economic growth, the nation's longest peacetime economic expansion, the 11.3 percent poverty rate for all persons in 2000 was still 0.2 percentage point above its 1973 historical low of 11.1 percent. The trend will undoubtedly be upward again with the mild recession of 2001. As explored in chapter 5, if the official family poverty thresholds had retained the same relationship to national median family income as they had in 1964, poverty rates today would still be as high as they were at the beginning of the War on Poverty. Thus, when consistently measured on a relative income basis, poverty has increased substantially in numbers without declining in proportions after nearly 40 years of antipoverty programs. This has occurred while the American gross domestic product was increasing by 224 percent in real terms (1964–2000) while the per capita real personal incomes of U.S. residents increased by 98 percent. That the developed world's highest relative poverty rate persists in the United States—the world's wealthiest nation—should be a cause of chagrin.

There continues to be a widely varying structure of poverty rates across demographic and socioeconomic subgroups. That U.S. poverty rates differ widely by age, race, ethnicity, and, in some cases, gender is a fact but not an explanation. Unless discrimination is inherent and persistent in the economic system, there must be other explanations as to why those differences persist. That poverty rates also differ by locality leaves an open question: in a world where brainpower counts more than mineral wealth or agricultural fertility in determining economic growth, why have the economies of those poorer locations not been more economically developed;

why have the people not moved to more economically favorable climes?

Family structure is, of course, a key factor, especially the continued growth in the numbers and proportions of female-headed families. But what are the causes of this feminization of poverty, and why cannot those rates be dampened or their consequences eased? Despite all the political rhetoric over family policies, why have we done so little to preserve married-couple families? Would a comprehensive set of economic and social policies aimed at restoring a family wage, providing allowances geared to the number of children and adults in the home, varying the size of the Earned Income Tax Credit (EITC) according to the number of parents, and increasing housing assistance for low-income, married-couple families help strengthen the institution of marriage? Staying together should be rewarded, and the failure to form a family unit or the fracturing of one when child well-being is at issue should carry more negative consequences. Why are society's efforts so limited when trying to extract from noncustodial parents their just share of the costs of caring for and preparing for life the children they so blithely participated in bringing into the world?

No more potentially profitable investment exists for society than the preparation of its next generation for a productive adulthood. Given that a substantial majority of the married mothers who have a choice have chosen to work at least part time prevents realistically asking whether the children of single parents would be better prepared if that single parent were compensated for full-time child rearing. It should be obvious that the well-being of future generations depends upon adequate family incomes, especially when the children in such families are quite young. When there is only one parent, if an adequate income is not to be provided by public assistance—as it never has been—it must come from the earnings of a parent adequately prepared for and provided with employment at family-sustaining earnings and provided with competent child care from some source. For those not potentially capable of such earnings from the regular labor market, whether one parent or two, there could be guaranteed public service employment, wage subsidies to employers to encourage their employment, and, as a last resort for those incapable of any work, cash transfers that would provide a family-sustaining income.

Some have argued that poverty is essential to capitalism, driven by the system's demand for cheap labor. That may be temporarily true in an emerging economy with primitive production methods and low labor productivity. But in a developed modern economy, cheap labor is generally accompanied by low profits. Low-wage production generally faces intense competition, especially from developing countries, low sales prices, and the barest of profit margins. The profitable firms of this day are those that prepare—or hire already prepared—those capable of operating sophisticated machinery or of carrying out human capital–intensive production of services or those possessed of unique personal skills resulting from high investment in human resources. These firms pay what is necessary to attract, adequately compensate, and retain workers with those unique skills. The sophisticated products and services of those forms of production then enter specialized markets at sales prices that generate the levels of profit that justify those investments. In the developed world, no one makes a significant profit from the maintenance of poverty, especially since so many of the official poor have limited attachment to the labor market.

Why then the persistence of poverty in the United States? The fact that so many developed countries with lower per capita gross domestic products (GDPs) have lower relative poverty rates than the United States indicates that the persistence is, at least in part, a matter of policy choice. There is no evidence that those more attractive poverty rates result from lower levels of unemployment or higher rates of productivity in those low-poverty countries. In recent years, quite the contrary has been the case, with the U.S. economy leading on both of these fronts. The fact of the matter is that greater willingness to share income more equitably pervades their systems more than ours. To a considerable extent, societies get the degrees of poverty and income inequality they desire.

However, in a sense, to donate to others an income they have not earned is not to have brought them out of poverty but rather to have helped them to survive more comfortably within it. For instance, if a homeless person were taken into a shelter and provided all of the desired food, clothing, and other amenities that, if purchased, would have required more than a poverty income, would that person be considered no longer poor? Only that income which can be attributed to a household's own efforts or sagacity can really be counted against their poverty. The United States can justifiably continue its reluctance to reward people with substantial unearned income only if it makes every reasonable effort to enable them to earn their own way out of poverty, including subsidized employment, while adequately providing unearned income to those who, for reasons such as disability or age, are not potentially capable of earning it.

What, then, would alleviate the persistence of poverty? A variety of macroeconomic policies, as well as micro-oriented economic, educational, housing, and nutrition policies and programs, could obtain substantial declines in the incidence of poverty. Among the most important macroeconomic determinants of family poverty in the United States since the late 1950s have been the pace of growth in real family incomes, unemployment rates, and the distribution of family incomes.[1] Strong growth in median family incomes and full employment in labor markets help raise those families above the existing poverty income threshold, provided that income inequality does not worsen, as it did from the mid-1970s through the mid-1990s. During the last half of the 1990s, a combination of steady growth in real family incomes, low unemployment, and a modestly improved family income distribution reduced the family poverty rate to a considerable degree. Debates remain over the renewed effectiveness of macroeconomic forces as antipoverty tools. Some argue that the strengthening of U.S. labor markets, rising real wages for low-wage workers, and expanded EITC credits played the dominant role, while others argue that national and state welfare reforms were the critical factors at work, encouraging more single mothers to work rather than receive welfare payments.[2]

Since, as noted in chapter 4, so much of poverty is inherited, it would be necessary to provide adequate prenatal care to ensure birth into good health and then to assure adequate personal development to overcome during childhood and youth the inherent disadvantages of birth into deprived circumstances, including cognitive, psychological, and nutritional disadvantages. Beyond healthy birth, the availability of adequate health care and nutrition throughout life is too essential to potential productivity to be left to the accidents of available family income. Sooner or later, health care in the United States must be, as public education is supposed to be, available regardless of household income. Medicare and Medicaid, including the State Child Health Insurance Program (SCHIP), are a good start, but they still leave far too many people outside and underserved.

Since family structure is so critical to the ability to earn adequate income and to care for children while doing so, far more effort is needed to maintain two-parent family unity as a matter of public policy. How often is the perceived inability to earn an adequate family income an excuse for a male's failure to undertake responsibility for family formation after an out-of-wedlock pregnancy or for the breakup of an existing marriage? Public policy can do much more to increase the earning capacity of any willing youth or adult, including greater investments in human capital, a more marriage-friendly earned income tax credit, and wage subsidies for low-income family heads favoring two-parent families. Because the ability to influence family stability by public policy has its limits, it is also necessary to insist on reasonable and persistent efforts to support any child one's actions have brought into the world. On the distaff side of the equation, the comment of Marion Wright Edelman of the Children's Defense Fund that "hope is the best contraceptive" expresses well the judgment that young women whose prospects are bright are not likely to risk them for an unpromising dalliance.[3]

Although the incidence of single parenthood and the poverty rate associated with it can be reduced, single parenthood is currently too ingrained in American society, as well as encouraged by certain elements of the national culture, to be diminished in a short time. The fact that so many dual-parent and single-parent mothers in families at all income levels work to sustain their families stands in the way of policies to pay low-income mothers to stay home, regardless of their motherhood capability. That, after all, was the basic issue of the 1996 welfare reform legislation. Therefore, the only reasonable solution is adequate employability development for those working mothers, supplemented amply by the Earned Income Tax Credit and other wage subsidies, while assuring competent child care within cost ranges commensurate with earning capacity and income.

The most effective antipoverty policy is, obviously, a combination of full employment and employability development, accompanied as needed by earnings supplements. If one examines existing antipoverty policies, however, those programs concerned with preparation for the labor market have the lowest relative funding levels. Instead, income maintenance and health care have had the highest per capita spending priority. The second-chance skill-training programs of the past 40 years have been of minor importance, overall, enrolling so few for such short training durations that they could never have a substantial effect on poverty rates, no matter how effectively they served their enrollees. The development of employability and the acquisition of human capital are a lifelong and multifaceted process. They involve the basic attitudes developed in childhood, including the degree of self-confidence and the enjoyment of accomplishment. They also involve the basic academic skills acquired from preschool on, the career awareness that awakens interest in the world of work, the career exploration that leads one to investigate potential alternatives, experimentation with work as occupational alternatives are tested and tentative career choices made, and career preparation and the accumulation of work experience, accompanied with adaptation to all of the changes that occur in a working career. Each of these steps can be affected to some extent by public policy. The single most important element is the acquisition of basic academic competence, which must be followed by sufficient education and skill training for long enough to create a worker who is among the more rather than the less prepared for jobs paying family-supporting wages. Even then, public policy must assure that such employment opportunities are available for those prepared for them, whether as a matter of macroeconomic policy or as direct job creation. Having all of those services in place would solve the poverty problem only for those motivated and logistically enabled to take advantage of the opportunities provided.

Suffice it to say that the persistence of poverty can be put on a long-term downward trajectory only through a range of policies assuring that those threatened by poverty have the opportunity for family-sustaining earnings, that over their lifetimes they are prepared for such employment, and that they are motivated to take advantage of these opportunities. Tracking the four-decade experience of U.S. antipoverty policy and recommending specific improvements in it is the burden of *Programs in Aid of the Poor*, to which the reader of this volume is encouraged to turn.[4] The understanding of poverty's persistence provided in this volume should make that resort more meaningful.

Notes

Chapter 1: The Rediscovery of Poverty

1. See Michael Harrington, *The Other America* (New York: Macmillan, 1962); Maurice Isserman, *The Other American: The Life of Michael Harrington* (New York: Public Affairs, 2000); Sar A. Levitan, *The Great Society's Poor Law* (Baltimore: Johns Hopkins Press, 1969); Robert Plotnick and Felicity Skidmore, *Progress against Poverty: A Review of the 1964–74 Decade* (New York: Academic Press, 1975).

2. Council of Economic Advisers, *Economic Report of the President, 1964* (Washington, D.C.: U.S. Government Printing Office, 1964); Robert Dalleck, *Flawed Giant: Lyndon Johnson and His Times, 1961–1973* (New York: Oxford University Press, 1968), 62.

3. Harrington, *The Other America.*

4. The Golden Era is typically defined as the 1946–73 period. For an overview of poverty developments during the Golden Era of the U.S. economy, see Sheldon Danzinger and Peter Gottschalk, *America Unequal* (Cambridge: Harvard University Press, 1995); Lowell E. Gallaway, *Poverty in America* (Columbus, Ohio: Grid, 1973); and Frank Levy, *Dollars and Dreams: The Changing American Income Distribution* (New York: Russell Sage Foundation, 1987).

5. Shortly thereafter, Victor Fuchs suggested a money income equal to one-half of the median income of families as the appropriate official definition of poverty. See Victor Fuchs, "Redefining Poverty and Redistributing Income," *Public Interest,* no. 8 (summer 1967): 88–95.

6. Timothy Smeeding, Lee Rainwater, and Gary Burtless, "United States Poverty in a Cross-national Context," *Focus* 21, no. 3 (2001): 50–54.

7. Sar Levitan et al., *Programs in Aid of the Poor,* 8th ed. (Baltimore: Johns Hopkins University Press, 2003).

Chapter 2: A Demographic Profile of the Nation's Poor

1. Daniel Patrick Moynihan, *Family and Nation* (New York: Harcourt, Brace, Jovanovich Publishers, 1987), 112.

2. Among the voluminous research studies examining the effects of

poverty on child outcomes are the following: Sharon Vandivere, Kristen Anderson Moore, and Brett Brown, "Child Well-being at the Outset of Welfare Reform: An Overview of the Nation and 13 States," in *Assessing the New Federalism,* Urban Institute (and Child Trends) B-23, November 2000; Jane Miller and Diane Davis, "Poverty History, Marital History, and Quality of Children's Home Environments," *Journal of Marriage and the Family* 59 (November 1997): 996–1007; Susan Mayer, "How Rich and Poor Children Differ," in *What Money Can't Buy* (Cambridge: Harvard University Press, 1997), 39–78; Children's Defense Fund, *Wasting America's Future: The Children's Defense Fund's Report on the Costs of Child Poverty* (Boston: Beacon Press, 1994); P. Nicholas Zill et al., "The Life Circumstances and Development of Children in Welfare Families: A Profile Based on National Data," in *Escape from Poverty: What Makes a Difference for Children,* ed. Lindsay Chase-Lansdale and Jeanne Brooks-Gunn (New York: Cambridge University Press, 1995), 38–59.

3. Robert Lerman, "The Impact of the Changing U.S. Family Structure on Child Poverty and Income Inequality," *Economica* 63, no. 250 (1996): S119–S139; Elizabeth Thomson, Thomas Hanson, and Sara McLanahan, "Family Structure and Child Well-being: Economic Resources vs. Parental Behaviors," *Social Forces* 73 (September 1994): 221–42.

4. See Ariel Halpern, "Poverty among Children Born outside of Marriage: Preliminary Findings from the National Survey of America's Families," in *Assessing the New Federalism,* Urban Institute Discussion Paper 99–16, December 1999.

5. For recent research on the antipoverty effects of child support income, see Elaine Sorenson and Chave Zibman, "Child Support Offers Some Protection against Poverty," in *Assessing the New Federalism,* Urban Institute B-10, March 2000; Daniel Mayer and Mei-Chen Hu, "A Note on the Antipoverty Effectiveness of Child Support among Mother-Only Families," *Journal of Human Resources* 34 (winter 1999): 225–34.

6. Based on their analysis of data from the National Survey of America's Families in 1997, Sorenson and Zibman found that child support income reduced the child poverty rate by 2 percentage points. See Sorenson and Zibman, "Child Support Offers Some Protection." Daniel Mayer and Mei-Chen Hu estimated that child support income raised 6–7% of poor, single-mother families out of poverty (Mayer and Hu, "Anti-poverty Effectiveness of Child Support").

7. Randy Capps, "Hardship among Children of Immigrants: Findings from the 1999 National Survey of America's Families," in *Assessing the New Federalism,* Urban Institute B-29, February 2001.

8. See Robert William Fogel, *The Fourth Great Awakening and the Future of Egalitarianism* (Chicago: University of Chicago Press, 2000); U.S. Census Bureau, "Historical Income Tables—Households," web site (www.census.gov), 2001.

9. See U.S. Department of Labor, Bureau of Labor Statistics, *Employment and Earnings,* January 1976, January 1996, and January 2001.

10. See Louis Harris and Associates, *Problems Facing Elderly Ameri-*

cans Living Alone, report prepared for the Commonwealth Fund Commission on Elderly People Living Alone, New York, 1986; Andrew Sum and Neal Fogg, "Labor Market and Poverty Problems of Older Workers and Their Families," in *Bridges to Retirement: The Changing Labor Market for Older Workers,* ed. Peter B. Doeringer (Ithaca: Cornell University Press, 1990), 33–63; Genaro C. Armas, "Older Women Face Greater Poverty Risk," *Boston Globe,* 1 November 2000.

11. Robert J. Lampman, "Population Change and Poverty Reduction, 1974–75," in *Poverty amid Affluence,* ed. Leo Fishman (New Haven: Yale University Press, 1966), 18–42.

12. U.S. Census Bureau, *Poverty in the United States, 1992* (Washington, D.C.: U.S. Government Printing Office, 1993); T. J. Eller, "Dynamics of Economic Well-being: Poverty, 1992–93: Who Stays Poor? Who Doesn't," Current Population Report P70–55 (Washington, D.C.: U.S. Government Printing Office, June 1996); Andrew Sum and Neeta Fogg, *The Income Inadequacy Problems of the Older Worker Population in Massachusetts: An Assessment of Recent Progress and Problems,* report prepared by the Massachusetts Blue Ribbon Commission on Older Workers, Boston, 1998; Eller, "Dynamics of Economic Well-being."

13. Eller, "Dynamics of Economic Well-being."

14. Hispanics can be members of any race.

15. For a review of key findings of the 2000 Census on the changing race-ethnic characteristics of the national population, see Cindy Rodriguez, "Latinos Surge in Census Count," *Boston Globe,* 8 March 2001; Genaro C. Armas, "Asian-American Population Surges," *Boston Globe,* 10 March 2001; Janny Scott, "Hispanics and Asians Fuel New Jersey's Population Growth," *New York Times,* 9 March 2001; Aaron Zitner, "Count: U.S. Has Twice as Many Undocumented Workers as Expected," *Los Angeles Times,* 9 March 2001.

16. For overviews of black economic progress in the United States in recent decades, see Gerald David Jaynes and Robin N. Williams, eds., *A Common Destiny: Blacks and American Society* (Washington, D.C.: National Academy Press, 1989); Reynolds Farley, *The New American Reality: Who We Are, How We Got Here, Where We Are Going* (New York: Russell Sage Foundation, 1996); Bart Landry, *The New Black Middle Class* (Berkeley and Los Angeles: University of California Press, 1987); U.S. Department of Commerce, "Census Bureau Releases Update on Country's African American Population," *U.S. Department of Commerce News,* February 2001; National Urban League, *State of Black America, 2001* (Washington, D.C.: National Urban League, 2001).

17. For a review of recent findings on the economic well-being of different Hispanic groups, including immigrants, see Juan Gonzales, *Harvest of Empire: A History of Latinos in America* (New York: Viking Penguin, 2000); Roberto Suro, *Strangers among Us: How Latino Immigration Is Transforming America* (New York: Alfred A. Knopf, 1998); Gregory Defreitas, *Inequality at Work: Hispanics in the U.S. Labor Force* (New York: Oxford University Press, 1999).

118 *Notes to Pages 27–29*

18. For ethnographic and city-specific case studies of white poverty, see Marc Pilsuk and Phyllis Pilsuk, *Poor Americans: How the White Poor Live* (Newark, N.J.: Transaction Books, 1971); Andrew Sum et al., *White Poverty in Boston* (Boston: Boston Foundation, 1993); Michael Patrick MacDonald, *All Souls: A Family Story from Southie* (Boston: Beacon Press, 1999).

19. These estimates are based on the March 2000 Current Population Survey (CPS) household survey and include as foreign-born those individuals who were born in the American Virgin Islands, Puerto Rico, Guam, or one of the other outlying territories of the United States. While immigrants from these areas are U.S. citizens, their entry into the United States increases the size of the resident population of the country.

20. Findings of the recently released 2000 Census data on the size of the resident population and the estimated undercount indicate that the population contained 7 million more individuals than previously estimated. Higher immigration flows were undoubtedly the key factor. See Andrew M. Sum et al., *An Analysis of the Preliminary 2000 Census Estimates of the Resident Population of the U.S. and Their Implications for Demographic, Immigration, and Labor Market Analysis and Policymaking,* Center for Labor Market Studies (Boston: Northeastern University, February 2001).

21. For two recent portraits of the foreign-born population of the United States in March 2000, see Steven A. Camorata, *Immigrants in the United States—2000: A Snapshot of America's Foreign Born Population* (Washington, D.C.: Center for Immigration Studies, January 2001); Lisa Lollock, *The Foreign-born Population in the United States, March 2000,* Current Population Reports, Series P-20, S34 (Washington, D.C., January 2001).

22. For an assessment of the demographic, economic, labor market, and social consequences of foreign immigration into the United States, see George J. Borjas, *Heaven's Door: Immigration Policy and the American Economy* (Princeton: Princeton University Press, 1999); James P. Smith and Barry Edmonston, eds., *The New Americans: Economic, Demographic, and Fiscal Effects of Immigration* (Washington, D.C.: National Academy Press, 1997); "Fixing Our Immigration Predicament," *American Enterprise* 11, no. 8 (2000): 14–37; Irwin M. Stelzer, "Immigration in the New Economy," *Public Interest* 141 (fall 2000): 5–16.

23. The definition of *native born* in the family poverty analysis follows that of most other analysts of CPS data. It includes all persons born in one of the 50 states or the District of Columbia, those born to U.S. citizens temporarily living abroad, and those born in Puerto Rico, Guam, or one of the other outlying territories of the United States.

24. For a review of the literacy and numeracy proficiencies of the native-born and foreign-born populations of the United States based on the National Adult Literacy Survey (NALS) and the International Adult Literacy Survey (IALS), see Irwin S. Kirsch et al., *Adult Literacy in America: A First Look at the Results of the National Adult Literacy Survey* (Washing-

ton, D.C.: National Center for Education Statistics, 1993); Andrew Sum, *Literacy in the Labor Force* (Washington, D.C.: National Center for Education Statistics, 1999); Sum et al., *Preliminary 2000 Census Estimates.*

25. A relatively high fraction of black immigrant family householders were four-year college graduates, and they were more likely to be married-couple families.

26. See Frederick Hollmann, Tammany J. Mulder, and Jeffrey E. Kallan, "Methodology and Assumptions for the Population Projections of the United States: 1999 to 2100," U.S. Census Bureau, Population Division Working Paper No. 38, 13 January 2000. For a critical assessment of these projections and their future demographic, economic, and environmental implications for the nation, see Leon Kolankiewicz, *Immigration, Population, and the New Census Bureau Projections* (Washington, D.C.: Center for Immigration Studies, June 2000).

27. Amy Borrus, "Workers of the World: Welcome," *Business Week,* 20 November 2000, 129–33.

28. See Ginger Thompson, "U.S. and Mexico to Open Talks on Free Migration for Workers," *New York Times,* 16 February 2001; Marion Lloyd, "Emigration Pays in Fox's Village," *Boston Globe,* 17 February 2001.

29. For an overview of findings on household living arrangements in 1990 and changes in household living arrangements during the 1990s, see Sam Roberts, *Who We Are: A Portrait of America* (New York: Random House, 1993); U.S. Census Bureau, *Marital Status and Living Arrangements: March 1998 Update,* Current Population Reports, Series P20, no. 514 (Washington, D.C.: U.S. Government Printing Office, 2000).

30. For a more detailed, historical view of trends in marriage, divorce, and separation in the United States, see Mary Jo Bane, *Here to Stay: Families in the Twentieth Century* (New York: Basic Books, 1976); Andrew J. Cherlin, *Marriage, Divorce, Remarriage* (Cambridge: Harvard University Press, 1981); Sar A. Levitan, Richard S. Belous, and Frank Gallo, *What's Happening to the American Family? Tensions, Hopes, Realities,* rev. ed. (Baltimore: Johns Hopkins University Press, 1988); Moynihan, *Family and Nation.*

31. The "unmarried" group includes individuals who are separated, divorced, and widowed, as well as those who were never married.

32. For a review of the changing household living arrangements and marital status of young adult men in the United States over the past few decades, see Clifford Johnson and Andrew Sum, *Declining Earnings of Young Men: Their Relation to Poverty, Teen Pregnancy, and Family Formation* (Washington, D.C.: Children's Defense Fund, 1987); Andrew M. Sum, Neal Fogg, and Robert Taggart, *Withered Dreams: The Decline in the Economic Fortunes of Young, Non–College Educated Male Adults and Their Families,* paper prepared for the William T. Grant Foundation Commission on Family Work and Citizenship, Washington, D.C., 1988; U.S. Census Bureau, "Young Adults Living at Home: 1960 to Present," web site (www.census.gov), January 2001.

33. The U.S. Census Bureau has estimated that the number of unmar-

ried-couple households has increased from only 523,000 in 1970 to 4.236 million in 1998. Nearly 36% of these households have one or more children under age 15 living in the home.

34. For a review of trends in the birthrates of young adult women in the United States and the share of births taking place out of wedlock during the 1990s, see *Facts at a Glance* (Washington, D.C.: Child Trends, December 1999); Andrew Sum, Neeta Fogg, and Garth Mangum, *Confronting the Youth Demographic Challenge: The Labor Market Prospects of Out-of-School Young Adults,* Sar Levitan Center for Social Policy Studies (Baltimore: Johns Hopkins University, October 2000); Stephanie Ventura et al., "Declines in Teenage Birth Rates, 1991–98: Update of National and State Trends," *National Vital Statistics Report* 47, no. 26 (1999).

Chapter 3: The Changing Geography of Poverty

1. Michael Harrington, *The Other America,* rev. ed. (Baltimore: Penguin Books, 1971), 2–3. The evolution of Harrington's views on poverty problems in the United States is described more fully in his biography; see Maurice Isserman, *The Other American: The Life of Michael Harrington* (New York: Public Affairs, 2000).

2. For a review of poverty and other economic problems in Appalachia in the early 1960s, see Harry M. Caudill, *Night Comes to the Cumberlands* (Boston: Atlantic-Little Brown, 1963); Mary Jean Bowman and W. Warren Haynes, *Resources and People in East Kentucky: Problems and Potentials of a Lagging Economy* (Baltimore: Johns Hopkins Press, 1963); Donald A. Crane and Benjamin Chinitz, "Poverty in Appalachia," in *Poverty amid Affluence,* ed. Leo Fishman (New Haven: Yale University Press, 1966), 124–49.

3. For a review of the Council of Economic Advisers's concepts and measures of poverty, see U.S. Council of Economic Advisers, *Economic Report of the President, 1964* (Washington, D.C.: U.S. Government Printing Office, 1964); Robert S. Lampman, "Population Change and Poverty Reduction, 1947–75," in *Poverty amid Affluence,* ed. Leo Fishman (New Haven: Yale University Press, 1966), 18–42.

4. For a review of regional variations in per capita incomes and family incomes during the 1980s and 1990s, see Cletus C. Coughlin and Thomas B. Mandelbaum, "Why Did Regional Per Capita Incomes Diverge in the 1980s?" *Federal Reserve Bank of St. Louis Review,* September/October 1988, 24–36; Frank Levy, *Dollars and Dreams: The Changing American Income Distribution* (New York: Russell Sage Foundation, 1987); Andrew Sum et al., *The State of the American Dream in New England* (Boston: Massachusetts Institute for a New Commonwealth, 1996); Andrew M. Sum et al., *The Northeast Region's Economy on the Eve of the Twenty First Century* (Washington, D.C.: John H. and Teresa Heinz Foundation, 2001); U.S. Congress, Joint Economic Committee, *The Bi-coastal Economy: Regional Patterns of Economic Growth during the Reagan Administration* (Washington, D.C., 1986).

5. Real output declines in the early 1990s were most severe in New England. See Paul Harrington and Andrew Sum, *The New England Economy in Recession: Its Economic and Social Consequences,* Center for Education and the Economy (Boston: Northeastern University, 1995).

6. See Andrew Sum with Ishwar Khatiwada and Sheila Palma, *Unprecedented Prosperity? Household Real Income Developments in the U.S. and Massachusetts in the 1990s* (Boston: Massachusetts Institute for a New Commonwealth, 2001).

7. See U.S. Census Bureau, *Poverty in the United States, 1999,* Current Population Reports, Consumer Income, Series P60–210, xii.

8. See Francis X. Clines, "Nation's Economic Boom a Faint Echo in Appalachia," *New York Times,* 5 July 1999; "Clinton in Poverty Tour Focuses on Profits," *New York Times,* 7 July 1999.

9. See Evelyn Nieves, "Forget Washington, the Poor Cope Alone," *New York Times,* 26 September 2000.

10. For a review of the initial farm/nonfarm adjustments to the family poverty income thresholds, see Mollie Orshansky, "Counting the Poor: Another Look at the Poverty Profile," *Social Security Bulletin,* January 1965.

11. For a review of the evidence, see Andrew M. Sum, Anwiti Bahuguna, and Sheila Palma with Paul Suozzo, *Housing Market Developments, Housing Cost Burdens, and the Cost of Living in Massachusetts and the Boston Metropolitan Area,* report prepared for the Teresa and H. John Heinz III Foundation and the Massachusetts Institute for a New Commonwealth, Boston, 1998.

12. Constance F. Citro and Robert T. Michael, eds., *Measuring Poverty: A New Approach* (Washington, D.C.: National Academy Press, 1995), 8, 195.

13. The economic development legislation included the Area Redevelopment Act of 1961 and the Appalachian Regional Development Act. See Sar A. Levitan, *Federal Aid to Depressed Areas: An Evaluation of the Area Redevelopment Administration* (Baltimore: Johns Hopkins Press, 1964); President's Appalachian Regional Commission, *Appalachia: A Report by the President's Appalachian Regional Commission, 1964* (Washington, D.C.: U.S. Government Printing Office, 1964); Donald A. Crane and Benjamin Chinitz, "Poverty in Appalachia," in *Poverty amid Affluence,* ed. Leo Fishman (New Haven: Yale University Press, 1966); Richard N. Goodwin, *Remembering America: A Voice from the Sixties* (Boston: Little, Brown, 1988).

14. See Robert Dalleck, *Flawed Giant: Lyndon Johnson and His Times, 1961–1973* (New York: Oxford University Press, 1998); Jules Witcover, *The Year the Dream Died: Revisiting 1968 in America* (New York: Warner Books, 1997); *Report of the National Advisory Commission on Civil Disorders* (New York: Bantam Books, 1968).

15. See William Julius Wilson, *The Truly Disadvantaged, the Inner City, the Underclass, and Public Policy* (Chicago: University of Chicago Press, 1987); Fred R. Harris and Roger W. Wilkins, eds., *Quiet Riots: Race*

and Poverty in the United States (New York: Pantheon, 1988); Christopher Jencks and Paul E. Peterson, eds., *The Urban Underclass* (Washington, D.C.: Brookings Institution, 1991); Erol R. Ricketts and Isabel V. Sawhill, "Defining and Measuring the Underclass," *Journal of Policy Analysis and Management* 7 (winter 1988): 316–25.

16. Poverty statistics on the urban and rural poor are available only from the decennial censuses. For a review of findings on the changing economics and demographics of nonmetropolitan and rural America, see Kenneth Johnson and Calvin L. Beale, "The Rural Rebound," *Wilson Quarterly* 22 (spring 1998): 16–27; Rob Gurwilt, "Keeping the Heart in the Heartland," *Wilson Quarterly* 22 (spring 1998): 28–41.

17. U.S. Census Bureau, *Poverty in the United States, 1999,* xiii.

18. See "A Conversation about Demography with Harold Hodgkinson," *Connection: New England's Journal of Higher Education and Economic Development,* summer 1999, 15–19.

19. The aggregate poverty data on central cities and suburbs for the 1989–99 period do not control for changes in the boundaries of cities and metropolitan areas over time or increases in the number of metropolitan areas. Nevertheless, the evidence is still striking.

20. Janice Madden's analysis of poverty trends in 181 metropolitan areas between 1980 and 1990 revealed a tendency for poverty to become more relatively concentrated in central cities. The higher the concentration in 1980, the greater the increase in concentration during the decade. See Janice F. Madden, *Changes in Income Inequality within U.S. Metropolitan Areas* (Kalamazoo: W. E. Upjohn Institute for Employment Research, 2000).

21. See William Julius Wilson, *The Truly Disadvantaged: The Inner City, the Underclass, and Public Policy* (Chicago: University of Chicago Press, 1987); William Julius Wilson, *When Work Disappears* (New York: Alfred Knopf, 1996); William J. Wilson, "Another Look at the Truly Disadvantaged," *Political Science Quarterly* 29 (winter 1991): 639–56; John D. Kasarda, "Structural Factors Affecting the Location and Timing of Urban Underclass Growth," *Urban Geography* 11 (May/June 1990); Lois Wacquant and William Julius Wilson, "Poverty, Joblessness, and the Social Transformation of the Inner City," in *Welfare Policy for the 1990s,* ed. Phoebe H. Cottingham and David T. Ellwood (Cambridge: Harvard University Press, 1989), 40–102.

22. See Jencks and Peterson, *The Urban Underclass;* Paul A. Jargowsky and Mary Jo Bane, "Ghetto Poverty in the United States, 1970–80," in ibid.; Ronald B. Mincey and Susan J. Weiner, *The Underclass in the 1980s: Changing Concepts, Constant Reality* (Washington, D.C.: Urban Institute, 1993).

23. The two other central cities outside of the Northeast and Midwest regions were Atlanta and Baltimore. See Jargowsky and Bane, "Ghetto Poverty in the United States."

24. See Paul A. Jargowsky, *Poverty and Place: Ghettos, Barrios, and the American City* (New York: Russell Sage Foundation, 1996).

25. The number of census tracts that were classified as high-poverty neighborhoods rose by 54% between 1980 and 1990. Ibid., 34.

26. Ibid., table 2–3, p. 41.

27. See William Julius Wilson, "When Work Disappears," *Political Science Quarterly* 111, no. 4 (winter 1996–97): 567–91.

28. For examples of such studies, see Jencks and Peterson, *The Urban Underclass;* Karen F. Parker and Matthew V. Pruitt, "Poverty, Poverty Concentration, and Homicide," *Social Science Quarterly* 81, no. 2 (2000): 555–70; Matthew R. Lee, "Concentrated Poverty, Race, and Homicide," *Sociological Quarterly* 41, no. 2 (2000): 189–206; "The State of the Nation's Cities," *Journal of Housing and Community Development* 55, no. 6 (1998): 24–30.

29. For examples of such studies, see Michelle Fine and Lois Weis, *The Unknown City: The Lives of Poor and Working-Class Young Adults* (Boston: Beacon Press, 1998); Le Alan Jones and Lloyd Newman with David Isay, *Our America: Life and Death on the South Side of Chicago* (New York: Scribner, 1997); David Simmon and Edward Burns, *The Corner: A Year in the Life of an Inner-City Neighborhood* (New York: Broadway Books, 1997); Michael Patrick MacDonald, *All Souls: A Family Story from Southie* (Boston: Beacon Press, 1999); Dalton Conley, *Honky* (Berkeley and Los Angeles: University of California Press, 2000).

30. One local drug dealer in South Chicago commented on his life chances in the following manner: "I ain't gonna be alive in ten years because I'll be selling my drugs and they're gonna pop my ass. No one's gonna be alive in twenty more years." See Jones and Newman, *Our America,* 45.

Chapter 4: The Causes of Poverty

1. Lawrence Mishel, Jared Bernstein, and John Schmitt, *The State of Working America, 2000–2001* (Ithaca: Cornell University Press, 2001).

2. For an overview of the findings of the empirical literature on the effects of children on labor force participation of women in the United States over the past 30 years, see William E. Bowen and Aldrich T. Finegan, *The Economics of Labor Force Participation* (Princeton: Princeton University Press, 1969); Ralph E. Smith, ed., *The Subtle Revolution: Women at Work* (Washington, D.C.: Urban Institute, 1979); James P. Smith, ed., *Female Labor Supply: Theory and Estimation* (Princeton: Princeton University Press, 1989); Francine D. Blau, Marianne Ferber, and Anne Winkler, *The Economics of Men, Women, and Work* (Upper Saddle River, N.J.: Prentice-Hall, 1998).

3. For analyses of the effects of young children on participation in the labor force, see Janis Barry Figueroa and Edwin Melendez, "The Importance of Family Members in Determining the Labor Supply of Puerto Rican, Black, and White Single Mothers," *Social Science Quarterly* 74, no. 4 (1993): 867–83; Neeta P. Fogg, "An Economic Analysis of the Determinants and the Long-Term Labor Market Consequences of Teenage Child-

bearing in the United States, 1979–1991" (Ph.D. diss., Northeastern University, Boston, 1997).

4. See Arleen Liebowitz and Jacob Klerman, "Explaining Changes in Married Mother's Employment over Time," *Demography* 32, no. 3 (1995): 365–78.

5. For evidence on this issue, see John Pencavel, "Labor Supply of Men: A Review," in *Handbook of Labor Economics,* ed. O. Ashenfelter and R. Layard (Amsterdam: North-Holland, 1986), vol. 1. More recent evidence for the 1990s using a model similar to that of Pencavel's yields very similar conclusions.

6. For alternative views on the role of the increased costs of children and changes in the taste for children on the fertility behavior of women in the United States in the past few decades, see Gary Becker, *A Treatise on the Family* (Cambridge: Harvard University Press, 1981); Susan Householder Van Horn, *Women, Work, and Fertility, 1900–1986* (New York: New York University Press, 1988).

7. For a comprehensive review of birthrates among teens and young adults and of the share of births taking place out of wedlock in the 1990s, see Andrew Sum, Neeta Fogg, and Garth Mangum, *Confronting the Youth Demographic Challenge: The Labor Market Prospects of Out-of-School Young Adults,* Sar Levitan Center for Social Policy Studies (Baltimore: Johns Hopkins University, October 2000).

8. For findings on the increasing feminization of poverty in the United States and in selected regions of the country in the 1970s and 1980s, see Jane Bayes, "Labor Markets and the Feminization of Poverty," in *Beyond Welfare: New Approaches to the Problem of Poverty in America,* ed. Harrel R. Rodgers Jr. (Armonk, N.Y.: M. E. Sharpe, 1988), 86–113; Victor Fuchs, *Poverty and Women* (Cambridge: National Bureau of Economic Research, 1986); Diana M. Pearce, "The Feminization of Ghetto Poverty," *Society* 1 (November–December 1983): 70–74; Andrew M. Sum et al., "Poverty amid Renewed Affluence: The Poor of New England at Mid-decade," *New England Journal of Public Policy* 2, no. 2 (1986): 6–31.

9. See Lowell Gallaway, *Poverty in America* (Columbus, Ohio: Grid, 1973), esp. "Poverty and Economic Growth," 43–60.

10. Among the studies on the link between economic growth and poverty in the 1970s, 1980s, and 1990s are Robert Haveman and Jonathan Schwabish, "Has Macroeconomic Performance Regained Its Antipoverty Bite?" *Contemporary Economic Policy,* October 2000, 415–27; Rebecca Blank, "Why Has Economic Growth Been Such an Ineffective Tool against Poverty in Recent Years?" in *Poverty and Inequality: The Political Economy of Redistribution,* ed. Jon Neill (Kalamazoo, Mich.: W. E. Upjohn Institute for Employment Research, 1997), 27–41; Rebecca Blank, "Why Were Poverty Rates So High in the 1980s?" National Bureau of Economic Research Working Paper 3878, October 1991.

11. Temporary Assistance to Needy Families (TANF) Program, Third Annual Report to Congress, U.S. Department of Health and Human Ser-

vices, Administration for Children and Families, Office of Planning, Research and Evaluation, Washington, D.C., August 2000.

12. For a review of the role of work incentives on employment decisions and poverty/dependency, see Gordon Berlin, "Welfare That Works: Lessons from Three Experiments That Fight Dependency and Poverty by Rewarding Work," *American Prospect,* 19 June–3 July 2000, 68–73; Kevin Duncan, "Incentives and Work Decisions of Welfare Recipients: Evidence from the Panel Survey of Income Dynamics, 1981–1988," *American Journal of Economics and Sociology* 59 (July 2000): 432–49; Rebecca Blank, "Fighting Poverty: Lessons from Recent U.S. History," *Journal of Economic Perspectives* 14, no. 2 (spring 2000): 3–19.

13. This estimate is based on published U.S. Census Bureau findings in *Poverty in the United States, 1999,* table 3, p. 180.

14. The low weekly earnings in retail trade are partly reflective of more frequent part-time employment. See U.S. Bureau of Labor Statistics, *Employment and Earnings,* March 2000, table B-2, 44–46.

15. For example, see Sar A. Levitan and Isaac Shapiro, *Working but Poor: America's Contradiction* (Baltimore: Johns Hopkins University Press, 1987); Marlene Kim, "Women Paid Low Wages: Who They Are and Where They Work," *Monthly Labor Review* 123, no. 9 (September 2000): 26–30; *Profile of the Working Poor, 1999,* U.S. Department of Labor, Bureau of Labor Statistics Report 947 (Washington, D.C.: U.S. Government Printing Office, February 2001).

16. See Andrew Sum, *Literacy in the Labor Force* (Washington, D.C.: National Center for Education Statistics, 1999).

Chapter 5: Approaches to and Consequences of Redefining Poverty

1. For earlier reviews of these critiques and recommendations for reform, see Constance F. Citro and Robert T. Michael, eds., *Measuring Poverty: A New Approach* (Washington, D.C.: National Academy Press, 1995); Neal Fogg, Andrew Sum, and Garth Mangum, *Poverty Ain't What It Used to Be: The Case for and Consequences of Redefining Poverty* (Baltimore: Sar Levitan Center for Social Policy Studies, Johns Hopkins University, 1999), esp. "Alternative Poverty Measures," chap. 2; Patricia Ruggles, *Drawing the Line: Alternative Poverty Measures and Their Implications for Public Policy* (Washington, D.C.: Urban Institute Press, 1990).

2. See U.S. Council of Economic Advisers, *Economic Report of the President, 1964* (Washington, D.C.: U.S. Government Printing Office, 1964).

3. See Mollie Orshansky, "Counting the Poor: Another Look at the Poverty Profile," *Social Security Bulletin* 28, no. 1 (1965): 3–29.

4. For an overview of the development and evolution of the poverty income thresholds of the federal government, see U.S. Department of Health, Education, and Welfare, *The Measuring of Poverty* (Washington, D.C.: U.S. Government Printing Office, 1976); Gordon M. Fisher, "The De-

velopment and History of the Poverty Thresholds," *Social Security Bulletin* 55, no. 4 (1997): 3–14.

5. The food spending multiplier of 3 was applied only to the food budgets of families containing three or more persons. A higher multiplier of 3.7 was used for generating a poverty threshold for two-person families, and the poverty line for a one-person household was based on the threshold for families of two.

6. For a more complete review of variations in family poverty thresholds by family size and the number of children under 18 in the family, see U.S. Census Bureau, *Poverty in the United States, 1999,* Consumer Income, Series P-60, no. 210 (Washington, D.C.: U.S. Government Printing Office, September 2000).

7. Citro and Michael, *Measuring Poverty,* 30.

8. For changes in the value of the national CPI-U over the period 1947–99, see U.S. Census Bureau, *Poverty in the United States, 1999,* Current Population Reports, Series P60, no. 210, table A-1, p. A-3.

9. For further details on the 1981 changes in the poverty concepts and measures, see Fisher, "History of the Poverty Thresholds."

10. The concepts of absolute and relative poverty are discussed at greater length in Bradley R. Schiller, *The Economics of Poverty and Discrimination,* 6th ed. (Englewood Cliffs, N.J.: Prentice Hall, 1995); Aldi J. M. Hagenaars, "The Definition and Measurement of Poverty," in *Economic Inequality and Poverty,* ed. Lars Osberg (Armonk, N.Y.: M. E. Sharpe, 1991), 134–56; Robert D. Plotnick and Felicity Skidmore, *Progress against Poverty: A Review of the 1964–1974 Decade* (New York: Academic Press, 1975); Peter Townsend, ed., *The Concept of Poverty* (London: Heinemann, 1970); Thesia I. Garner et al., "Experimental Policy Measurement in the 1990s," *Monthly Labor Review* 121, no. 3 (March 1998): 39–61; Citro and Michael, *Measuring Poverty.*

11. The description by Orshansky of the poverty income thresholds as a "relative absolute" measure of poverty is cited in Fisher, "History of the Poverty Thresholds," 6.

12. See Citro and Michael, *Measuring Poverty.*

13. See Dean Baker, *Getting Prices Right: The Debate over the Consumer Price Index* (Washington, D.C.: Economic Policy Institute, 1998); John M. Berry, "CPI Report Coming under Fire," *Washington Post,* December 1996; James Devine, "The Cost of Living and Hidden Inflation," *Challenge* 44, no. 2 (March–April 2001): 73–84; Daniel Mitchell, "Calculating the Price of Everything: The CPI," *Challenge* 41, no. 5 (1998): 99–112; "Measuring the CPI, a Symposia," *Journal of Economic Perspectives* 12, no. 1 (1998): 3–78.

14. Fogg et al., *Poverty Ain't What It Used to Be,* xi.

15. See Citro and Michael, *Measuring Poverty;* Andrew Sum and Anwiti Bahuguna with Sheila Palma, *Rethinking Poverty Measures, Local Housing Costs, Adjusted Poverty Lines, and Their Consequences for Massachusetts* (Boston: Massachusetts Institute for a New Commonwealth, 1998); Fogg et al., *Poverty Ain't What It Used to Be.*

16. See U.S. Bureau of Labor Statistics, *Consumer Expenditures in 1999* (Washington, D.C.: U.S. Government Printing Office, 21 December 2000).

17. See U.S. Department of Housing and Urban Development, "Fair Market Rents for Fiscal Year 2001, Final Rule," *Federal Register* 65, no. 186 (25 September 2000): 57658–57717.

18. Thesia I. Garner et al., "Experimental Policy Measurement in the 1990s," *Monthly Labor Review* 121, no. 3 (March 1998): 39–61.

19. For a review of the purposes of the BLS family budgets and the methods used to generate their values, see U.S. Bureau of Labor Statistics, *BLS Handbook of Methods,* Bulletin 1910 (Washington, D.C.: U.S. Government Printing Office, 1976). The U.S. Bureau of Labor Statistics also produced equivalence scales that could be used by researchers to determine the annual amount of income needed by urban families of varying sizes and age compositions to achieve each of the three budget standards. These data could be used to identify the share of a given metro area's households and families who had incomes high enough to achieve each of the three budget standards. See U.S. Bureau of Labor Statistics, *Revised Equivalence Scale for Estimating Equivalent Incomes or Budget Cost by Family Type* (Washington, D.C.: U.S. Government Printing Office, 1968).

20. See U.S. Department of Labor, Employment and Training Administration, "Workforce Investment Act: Lower Living Standard Income Level," Washington, D.C., 3 May 2001.

21. See Adam Smith, *An Inquiry into the Nature and Consequences of the Wealth of Nations* (Washington, D.C.: Regnery Publishing, 1998), 999.

22. See Peter Townsend, "The Meaning of Poverty," *British Journal of Sociology* 13 (1962): 210–27. For a review of the debates over the comparative merits of an absolute and relative income approach to poverty, see Amartya Sen, "Poverty, Relatively Speaking," *Oxford Economic Papers* 35 (1983): 153–69; Peter Townsend, "A Sociological Approach to the Measurement of Poverty—a Rejoinder to Professor Amartya Sen," *Oxford Economic Papers* 37 (1985): 659–68; Amartya Sen, "A Sociological Approach to the Measurement of Poverty: A Reply to Professor Peter Townsend," *Oxford Economic Papers* 37 (1985): 669–76.

23. See Victor R. Fuchs, "Redefining Poverty and Redistributing Income," *Public Interest,* no. 8 (summer 1967), 88–95.

24. See Robert M. Solow, "Welfare: The Cheapest Country," *New York Review of Books* 47, no. 5 (23 March 2000): 20–24.

25. Citro and Michael, *Measuring Poverty.*

26. In March 2000, there were only 477,000 families in the United States with eight or more persons. They, thus, represented only two-thirds of 1% of all family households in the nation at that time.

27. For a review of alternative subjective definitions and measures of poverty in the United States and other nations, see Ruggles, *Drawing the Line;* Karel Vanden Bosch et al., "A Comparison of Poverty in Seven European Countries and Regions, Using Subjective and Relative Measures," *Journal of Population Economics* 6, no. 3 (1993): 235–59; Aldi J. M. Hage-

naars, "The Definition and Measurement of Poverty," in *Economic Inequality and Poverty: International Perspectives,* ed. Lars Osberg (Armonk, N.Y.: M. E. Sharpe, 1991), 134–56; Andrew Sum et al., *White Poverty in Boston* (Boston: Boston Foundation, 1993); Citro and Michael, *Measuring Poverty.*

28. For some of these surveys, see William O'Hare et al., *Real Life Poverty in America: Where the American Public Would Set the Poverty Line* (Washington, D.C.: Center on Budget and Public Policy Priorities and Families USA Foundation, July 1990); Andrew Sum, Neal Fogg, and Neeta Fogg, *Income and Employment Problems of Families in Boston's Low Income Neighborhoods* (Boston: Center for Labor Market Studies, 1990), 77–82; Andrew Sum, Ted Murphy, and Tom Maher, *The Dream: Deferred or Denied?* (Boston: Community Jobs Collaborative and Center for Labor Market Studies, 1989).

29. See S. Anna Kondratas, "The Problems of Measuring Poverty," in *Economics 86/87,* eds. Reuben Slesinger and Glen Beeson (Guildford, Conn.: Dushkin Publishing Group, 1987), 86–94; Charles Murray, "The War on Poverty: 1965–1980," *Wilson Quarterly* 8, no. 4 (autumn 1984): 94–113; Andrew Sum et al., *The State of the American Dream in New England* (Boston: Massachusetts Institute for a New Commonwealth, 1996); Ron Haskins, "The Verdict on Welfare Reform," *Weekly Standard,* 13 November 2000.

30. See U.S. Census Bureau, *Poverty in the United States, 1999,* Current Population Reports, Consumer Income, Series P60–210; U.S. Census Bureau, "Poverty 1998: People in Poverty by Definition of Income and Selected Characteristics," U.S. Census Bureau web site (www.census.gov); U.S. Census Bureau, "Historical Poverty Tables—Poverty by Definition by Income (R&D)," U.S. Census Bureau web site (www.census.gov).

31. In their analysis of the data from the National Survey of America's Families, several Urban Institute researchers have used 200% of the official poverty line as their poverty criterion. See Gregory Acs, Katherin Ross Phillips, and Daniel McKenzie, *Playing by the Rules but Losing the Game: America's Working Poor* (Washington, D.C.: Urban Institute, May 2000).

32. For a similar exercise estimating the effects of alternative definitions of the working poor in the United States, see ibid. When the income criterion for defining the poor is raised to twice the poverty line, the authors find that the number of persons in families where the average adult worked at least 1,000 hours increases by a multiple of 4.

33. The finding of a lower incidence of income inadequacy problems among families with a nonemployed householder than among families whose head worked between 1 and 26 weeks is attributable to the behavior of the elderly. The nonelderly who failed to work during the year were more likely to be poor than their counterparts with some work experience.

34. See Internal Revenue Service, *2000 Form 1040, Forms and Instructions* (Washington, D.C., 2001). A single individual or a family with no eligible children with earnings under $10,400 is potentially eligible for an EIC payment up to a maximum of $353.

35. For a more detailed discussion of the methods used to estimate the fungible value of Medicare and Medicaid benefits and the value of public and subsidized rental housing, see U.S. Bureau of the Census, *Measuring the Effects of Benefits and Taxes on Income and Poverty, 1992,* Current Population Reports, Series P60–186 RD (Washington, D.C.: U.S. Government Printing Office, 1993).

36. See Thomas M. Beers, "Profile of the Working Poor, 1999," U.S. Bureau of Labor Statistics Report 947 (Washington, D.C., February 2001).

37. Robert Haveman and Lawrence Buron, "Escaping Poverty through Work: The Problem of Low Earning Capacity in the United States, 1973–88," *Review of Income and Wealth* 39 (June 1993): 141–57.

Chapter 6: Is Poverty in the United States Inescapable?

1. For earlier studies of the links between economic growth, income distribution, and poverty, see Rebecca M. Blank and Alan S. Blinder, "Macroeconomics, Income Distribution, and Poverty," in *Fighting Poverty,* ed. Sheldon H. Danziger and Daniel H. Weinberg (Cambridge: Harvard University Press, 1996); Eugene Smolensky et al., "Growth, Inequality, and Poverty: A Cautionary Note," *Review of Income and Wealth* 40, no. 2 (1994): 217–22; Robert Haveman and Jonathan Schwabish, "Has Macroeconomic Performance Regained Its Antipoverty Bite?" *Contemporary Economic Policy* 18, no. 4 (2000): 415–27.

2. See Joseph Holtz, Charles Mullin, and John Karl Scholz, "The Earned Income Tax Credit and Employment among Families on Welfare," *Poverty Research News,* Joint Center for Poverty Research, May–June 2001, 13–15; June O'Neill and M. Anne Hill, *Gaining Ground? Measuring the Impact of Welfare Reform on Welfare and Work,* Manhattan Institute for Policy Research, New York, 2001; James P. Zillak et al., "Accounting for the Decline in AFDC Caseloads: Welfare Reform or the Economy," *Journal of Human Resources* 35, no. 3 (2000): 570–86.

3. Marion Wright Edelman, quoted in Public/Private Ventures, *Youth Development Issues: Challenges and Directions* (Philadelphia: Public/Private Ventures, 2000), 28.

4. Sar Levitan et al., *Programs in Aid of the Poor,* 8th ed. (Baltimore: Johns Hopkins University Press, 2003).

Index